e

Music

Went

'Round

and

Around

The Music Went 'Round and Around

The Story of MUSICARNIVAL

John Vacha

The Kent State University Press   Kent and London

© 2004 by The Kent State University Press, Kent, Ohio 44242
ALL RIGHTS RESERVED
ISBN 0-87338-798-8
Library of Congress Catalog Card Number 2003028275
Manufactured in the United States of America

08   07   06   05   04   5   4   3   2   1

LIBRARY OF CONGRESS CATALOGING-IN-PUBLICATION DATA
Vacha, John.
    The music went 'round and around : the story of Musicarnival / John Vacha.
          p.   cm.
    Includes bibliographical references and index.
    ISBN 0-87338-798-8 (pbk. : alk. paper)
    1. Musicarnival (Warrensville Heights, Ohio)
    2. Musical theater—Ohio—Cleveland—History.
I. Title.
    ML1711.8.C57V3 2004
    782.1'079'77131—dc22
          2003028275

British Library Cataloging-in-Publication data are available.

To the memory of
My Mother and Father:
Norma S. and Edward O. Vacha

Contents

Preface: Welcome to Musicarnival!

Whenever I think of *South Pacific*, I visualize it in the round. The Rodgers and Hammerstein characters populate a circular, nearly bare stage, symbolic of the lonely island on which the action takes place. They are surrounded on all sides by an unbroken sea—the faces of the audience. I first saw *South Pacific*, of course, at Musicarnival.

Along with an entire generation of Clevelanders, I saw quite a few classics of the American musical stage for the first time at Musicarnival. For those of us who missed the touring New York companies at the Hanna Theatre, John Price's tent theater in Warrensville Heights more often than not gave us our next chance to catch those shows in a professional production. It first opened its flaps in 1954, during the golden age of the American musical, and kept its pennant fluttering above the "Queen of the Big Tops" for the following twenty-two summers. In many respects, the history of Musicarnival, especially for the production years, is the history in microcosm of that original American art form.

Although theater is probably the most collaborative of art forms, any history of Musicarnival is to a large degree a biography of its

South Pacific proved to be the most popular show of Musicarnival's production years. Seabees shown here in the 1965 revival lament that "There Is Nothing Like a Dame." Set on a "lonely island" during World War II, it was an ideal musical for arena staging. John L. Price Jr. Musicarnival Archives, Cleveland Public Library.

founder and guiding genius, John L. Price Jr. The full list of his credits would include a great many of the significant theatrical enterprises of his era in Cleveland, but Musicarnival is the connective tissue that binds them all together. Fortunately he was also a saver, and the John L. Price Jr. Musicarnival Archives provide as rich a documentary record as left by any local theater.

In undertaking this history of Musicarnival, then, I am indebted first and foremost to John Price for donating his archives to the Cleveland Public Library. Next, Mrs. Evelyn Ward and the staff of that institution's literature department made those materials available in record time and were unfailingly accommodating and helpful to me in my research. Retired theater librarian Herbert Mansfield provided greatly appreciated guidance through the picture and slide collection.

Several people helped fill in, elucidate, and complement the printed record by sharing their memories of Musicarnival through oral interviews, including those of John Price, William Boehm, Diana Price, Jock Price, Frank Baloga, and Keith Joseph. Quotations taken from these interviews may be recognized by verbs of attribution in the present tense. I am grateful moreover to Diana Price for reviewing the manuscript in the interest of accuracy. Final responsibility for accuracy of fact as well as opinion rests, as always, with the author.

Finally, I would like to thank the editors and staff of the Kent State University Press for their encouragement in inaugurating this series on individual Cleveland theaters as an extension of our general history, *Showtime in Cleveland*. Thanks also to my wife, Ruta, for continued patience and support, and to my niece, Audrey Dadzitis Hopkins, for putting me right with the computer age.

And now, settle back in your canvas deck chair as the house lights dim. If you're on the aisle, you may feel a sudden stir of warm summer air as a figure races past from the back of the house and bounds confidently up onto the white stage. A young man in a crew cut and red blazer peers out at that encircling sea of faces and addresses them in a ringing tenor: "Good evening, neighbors, and welcome to Musicarnival!"

"Price's Folly"

During the spring of 1954 a young Navy veteran suddenly began hanging around the racetrack. His mother, Emma Price, and his wife, Connie, were not overly concerned; they knew that Johnny Price wasn't smitten by the ponies. Both had had their flings with the stage, and they knew that John was simply incurably stagestruck. Where railbirds watched thoroughbreds rounding the final turn into the homestretch, Price envisioned chorus girls breaking into their routines just beyond the oval rail.

What Price had in mind for the northwestern corner of the Thistledown grounds near the intersection of Warrensville Center and Emery Roads was a new and unique summer theater. Inspired by a recent trend on the East Coast, he planned to produce musical shows under a huge, circuslike tent. The big-top imagery would inspire, or more accurately necessitate, the adoption of another contemporary theatrical trend. In the tradition of Ringling Brothers and other circus impresarios, Price would be staging his shows on a circular platform right in the middle of his audience—in the round.

Summer theaters in themselves were nothing new in the Cleveland theatrical tradition. Nearly a century earlier, Clevelanders had begun patronizing Haltnorth's Gardens on Kinsman Road. At first this was a simple German beer garden, viewed suspiciously by the earlier settlers with their New England Congregational origins. The *Cleveland Leader* in 1863 labeled it the city's greatest nuisance, a gathering place for pickpockets, prostitutes, and "shoulder hitters" (whatever that was—perhaps nineteenth-century slang for purse snatchers). By 1872, after its relocation at Willson (East 55th) and Woodland Avenue, Haltnorth's had become a widely popular gathering place with spacious grounds laid out around a picturesque pond. One of its chief attractions was a theater that featured concerts and operettas by the Holman Opera Company, among others. All the popular Gilbert and Sullivan shows, from *H.M.S. Pinafore* to *Patience,* could be seen there in the 1880s and 1890s.

There was even a summer tent theater in the city's past. The Cleveland Pavilion Theater flourished in the 1880s between Wood (East 4th) and Bond (East 6th) Streets, probably in the old Lake View Park, descending from the bluffs to the railroad tracks along Lake Erie. It could accommodate up to two thousand spectators under canvas to view musical productions such as *The Chimes of Normandy.*

With the turn of the century, summer theatrics shifted to the Euclid Avenue Garden Theater, which opened in 1904 at Euclid Avenue and Kennard (East 40th) Street. Unlike Haltnorth's, these gardens were described by a patron, Edith Moriarty, as "a temperance theater." Moriarty recalled, "Green grass and trees, tables, umbrellas and chairs, invited the audience, particularly the young girls on Saturday afternoons, spending their allowances on the matinee, with sodas and root beer between the acts." There was a stuccoed pavilion of Spanish Moorish design set two hundred feet back from the street, open to the air on three sides, and facing the stage on the fourth. Typical of the musical fare was Gilbert and Sullivan's *The Mikado.* By World War I, however, the Euclid Avenue Gardens had given way to the commercial redevelopment of their eponymous street.

More permanent than any of these predecessors and a direct precursor to Musicarnival was Cain Park. This began with the joint inspiration of Cleveland Heights Mayor Frank Cain and Dr. Dina Rees

Evans, a dramatics teacher at Cleveland Heights High School. Evans started out by requesting permission to use a natural ravine at Superior Avenue and Taylor Road for an outdoor production of *A Midsummer Night's Dream* in 1934. Mayor Cain not only granted approval but also subsequently promoted construction of a permanent amphitheater on the site. Built partially with labor from the New Deal's Works Progress Administration (WPA), Cain Park formally opened in 1938 as the country's first municipally owned outdoor theater.

Under the direction of "Doc" Evans, Cain Park became the area's preeminent summer theater and provided many of its fondest memories over the following decade. Repertoire ranged from classics such as *Peer Gynt* to such recent Broadway hits as *Arsenic and Old Lace*. But operettas soon became the three-thousand-seat, open-air theater's forte, exemplified by productions of *The Chocolate Soldier, The Vagabond King, Naughty Marietta,* and *The Student Prince,* among other chestnuts. Not even obstacles such as the occasional rainout or lack of parking facilities could keep the crowds away. Nor could they keep away the annual migration of theater hopefuls from across the country. Through the years, names such as Hal Holbrook, Jack Lee, Pernell Roberts, and Dom DeLuise joined Cain Park's roster of distinguished alumni.

Other than Evans herself, no one could claim a closer bond with Cain Park than John Price. His mother had a leading role, along with Dorothy Fuldheim, in the theater's first dramatic production of *The Warrior's Husband* in 1938. From Cassius in *Julius Caesar* to the Indian in *High Tor,* Price himself had a part in every Cain Park production during the first ten years, except during his stint in the service. Through sheer force of habit, Price recalls, "I would call Musicarnival 'Cain Park' for several years."

Price was a local product all the way, a fourth-generation Clevelander. He was the son of John Lemar Price, a stockbroker who could quote Shakespeare and other poets by the hour—a trait he passed on to his second son. As for the stage itself, although he was distantly related to actress Agnes Moorehead, the elder Price limited himself to walk-on parts at Cain Park.

During his four-year run as Mr. Weather-Eye on television station WEWS, John Price was visited by a notable cousin on his father's side, actress Agnes Moorhead. Following Musicarnival's successful debut year, Price bid goodbye to his day job on television. *Cleveland Press* Collection.

It was his mother, Emma Moskopp Price, who more likely transmitted thespian genes to John Lemar Price Jr. She had been president of the Dramatic Club at Flora Stone Mather College and a charter member of the alumnae group's College Club Players. After her marriage, she gave talks on modern drama, helped start a dramatics group of the Women's Civic Club of Cleveland Heights, and served on the original Mayor's Committee for Cain Park. Emma got the whole family involved in the latter venture, as her husband joined her in bit parts and her older son Robert worked with the stage crew.

As for Johnny, he considered his exposure to Evans at Cleveland Heights High School to have been one of the luckiest breaks of his life. Naturally he was a member of the Heights Players, and when he graduated in 1938 he was named most likely to succeed. That summer he became one of the original "Doc Evans's boys" during the inaugural season of Cain Park, playing the role of Watt in *Sherwood*.

Western Reserve University didn't yet have a drama major in 1938, so Price majored in speech and took all the courses he could in the school's fledgling theater program. There he studied under the program's founder, Barclay Leathem, and directors Nadine Miles and Edwin Duerr, appearing in Eldred Theatre's productions of August Strindberg's *The Spook Sonata* (a Leathem obsession), Clifford Odets's *Rocket to the Moon,* and Thornton Wilder's *The Merchant of Yonkers* (later to be resuscitated as *The Matchmaker* and even later as *Hello, Dolly!*). Among his classmates were Bill Boehm from John Adams High School and Martin Fuss from Glenville, who would later rule Hollywood as Ross Hunter. During the summers all three would join Doc Evans's boys at Cain Park, where Price's characterizations ranged from young Howie Newsome in *Our Town* to old Gramp Maple in *The Petrified Forest.*

Taking his degree shortly after Pearl Harbor, Price immediately found employment in the U.S. Navy. As a lieutenant in the naval amphibious forces, he commanded an LST (officially, Landing Ship Tank; unofficially, Large Slow Target) in the second wave to hit Utah Beach on D-Day. Writing to Evans, Price inevitably described the spectacle in theatrical terms: "I've been right in the front row watching my own little show. I may even say that I have been backstage and at times on stage, especially at the rising of the curtain and was it ever an exciting opening." His landing craft took so many hits it never made it back to England, being abandoned midway in the process of getting towed back across the channel.

Cleveland drama critic Peter Bellamy once described Price as "a mercurial mixture of charmer and fighter, extrovert and introvert, actor and businessman, the flamboyant and the sensitive," a formula neatly reduced by the headline writer to "No shrinking violet." Most of these qualities and a few more were employed in Price's next World War II exploit, his celebrated unauthorized expedition to Paris.

Although outfitted back in Southampton with a new LST through some snafu in naval red tape, Price and his crew were idly sitting in it with no orders. Meanwhile the radio brought news that Paris was in the process of being liberated. Paris sounded like the place to be, so Price and crew simply took their ship back to France, landing on a British-controlled beach where they were benignly ignored as "crazy Americans." Leaving a corporal's guard on the LST, the others took off for the once and future City of Light, splitting up and arranging to meet at a later time on the steps of the Paris Opera. Price hailed the first American vehicle he saw and unbelievably discovered fellow Cain Parker Pat O'Keefe behind the wheel. He rode into "Paree" on the spare tire fixed to the running board, not minding "the sorest butt you ever saw."

"Oh, me, oh, my. Cleveland was never like this," Price wrote of their reception in another letter to Evans. "The girls, mothers, grandmothers, even the men kissed us. . . . We were all over lipstick." Price used his high school French to tell the crowds how grateful they were for the welcome, adding, "We thought their women to be smarter and better looking than any in the world (which, by God they are), and that we thought that Paris was the most beautiful city in the world (which it simply must be)."

Bivouacking at the Grand Hotel, which refused their money, Price and O'Keefe went out on their balcony for more oratory when they sensed "a weird, electric groundswell of feeling" in the street. They went back out to join an impromptu procession down the Champs Elysee, walking arm-in-arm with the Parisians and singing "La Marseillaise." The flow took them to the Arch de Triomphe, where they witnessed the relighting of the flame on the tomb of France's Unknown Soldier. "No greater thrill could be experienced," he wrote Evans, apologizing for the "overdose" of exclamation points. "What luck. Oh, man, oh man, oh man!!!!"

That was a tough act to follow, but Price came home after demobilization determined to top it in the postwar theater. He went back to Cain Park, where he broadened his experience as producer, director, and performer on the Cain Park Theatre of the Air over radio stations WGAR and WHK. A newer and more transient venue was the Ring Theater, which an actor-entrepreneur named Ray Boyle rigged up over the swimming pool in the Allerton Hotel on East 13th Street. There he acted briefly opposite a young lady named Ann Corio, whose path in show business would recross his many years later. Price also began to appear on the stage of the venerable Cleveland Play House, where he encountered another young woman who would play a much more immediate role in his life.

Her name was Constance Mather, and though Bostonian by birth she had strong local connections. Her father, Philip, was one of *the* Mathers and consequently a director of the Cleveland Cliffs Iron Company. Thus she was no stranger to Cleveland, and the Mathers were even acquainted with the Prices. Connie and John had never met, however, not even when she had been dispensing coffee and doughnuts for the Red Cross to American troops in England during the war. Her interest in theater led her to the Cleveland Play House, and to John Price, in the autumn of 1946.

She had the cool beauty of a debutante with the poised elegance of an experienced horsewoman. He combined the tanned good looks of a Navy veteran with a deep smile that engaged his entire face. They were married the following year.

In his efforts to make a living in show business, Price began to divide his time between Cleveland and New York. He picked up work in network radio, appearing on *The Bob Hope Show, The Gene Autry Show,* and especially on *Duffy's Tavern* with Ed Gardner, where he played character roles and served as stage manager. However, when Gardner made plans to broadcast from Puerto Rico for the tax breaks, Price returned to Cleveland.

A new entertainment medium began in Cleveland with the introduction of television station WEWS in 1947. Price was hired by the city's second station, WNBK (now WKYC), which made its debut on October 31, 1948. There he wrote, directed, and produced such shows as *The Troubadour, Rowena, The Minstrel Girl,* and *Golden Wedding.* His efforts to protect his performers led to clashes with the engineers' union, however, a battle in which Price came out on the losing end.

Returning to live theater, Price picked up some work at the Hanna Theatre as a supernumerary in touring Broadway shows. When Hanna manager Milton Krantz built a production of *The Man Who Came to Dinner* around the Sheridan Whiteside of former Cleveland Indians owner Bill Veeck, Price landed the part of the antic Banjo. Around the corner from the Hanna, Price also began working at Herman Pirchner's Playhouse Square nightspot, the Alpine Village. There he devoted his talents to adapting, producing, and directing capsule versions of popular operettas and musicals, often appearing in them with his fraternity brother and Cain Park colleague, Bill Boehm.

In 1951 the hot show on Broadway was Frank Loesser's *Guys and Dolls,* and Price drew the assignment of pirating the show's plot and songs for the Alpine Village. "I paid to see the first and second acts six or seven times, but knew the second act better because I walked in so many times after intermission without paying," he later confessed. Given his intense exposure to the show, Price was bound to either love it or loathe it; happily, it became one of his perennial favorites. Loesser, hearing of the theft, wasn't at all happy, but his reported threats to bring suit were never carried through.

Then Price found himself back in television again when he landed the role of Mr. Weather-Eye for WEWS. His Navy crew cut fit the Ivy League image the station was looking for, he explained, and it didn't hurt too that he had once acted with the sponsor's daughter—at Cain Park, naturally. Price performed his daily five-minute stint for several years, appearing next to Cleveland television icon Dorothy Fuldheim and coming up with his signature salutation, "Good evening, neighbors." It provided him with the financial security he needed for his growing family, which now included son Jock and daughter Diana. It also gave him enough free time to make plans for his ultimate ambition—a theater of his own.

Ideally, Price would have liked to establish a small theater for classical drama and new scripts. "But I was practical enough to know that I couldn't do classical drama in Cleveland, Ohio," he says. Then he ran into Boehm, who had just done *The Student Prince* in Skaneateles, New York, in the Finger Lakes region. The show was performed in a tent. "Bill extolled the virtues of these musical tents and predicted that they would be the wave of the future for American summer stock," Price says, and he became an eager convert.

The idea was both as old as the Roman circus and as contemporary as the Second World War. An actor and adventurer with the swashbuckling name of St. John Terrell was responsible for its postwar reincarnation. Born in Chicago, Terrell broke into show business with a fire-eating act in a local carnival. Later he was heard on network radio as the title character on *Jack Armstrong, the All-American Boy.* During World War II, "Sinjun" (as he was called) landed in a USO troupe in the Philippines. When a touring company of Irving Berlin's *This Is the Army* couldn't find a suitable stage in Manila, Terrell proposed scooping out a natural bowl with some bulldozers, pitching a tent over it, and staging the show in the middle, with the GI audience seated around the periphery. The idea was strangled by Army red tape.

Back home Terrell followed through on his own by opening the Music Circus in 1949 in Lambertville, New Jersey, with a production of *The Merry Widow.* Music Circus was located on the Delaware River, about twenty miles north of Philadelphia, and financed in part by Terrell's Army craps winnings and the family perfume business. The novelty quickly attracted a broad, popular following. "The tent reduces the country people's distrust of the theater's forbidding formalities," he explained. "The wise guys enjoy the new twist we give the old standbys."

Success bred the usual imitators. Terrell himself established the Treasure Island Music Circus in Miami Beach, Florida, and assumed management of the Neptune Music Circus in Asbury Park, New Jersey. There were nine of these theaters by 1954, including Melody Fair in Toronto, the Cape Cod Music Circus in Hyannis, Massachusetts, and the Finger Lakes Lyric Circus in Skaneateles, New York.

Initially reluctant to get involved in show business, attorney Robert Bishop III (left), another Price cousin, finally took the plunge and became Musicarnival's president and a leader in the music-tent phenomenon. He and publicist Marsh Samuel even got into the act with cameo appearances as swimmers in the Musicarnival production of *Wish You Were Here*. John L. Price Jr. Musicarnival Archives, Cleveland Public Library.

(A visit to the Toronto operation had inspired Tyrone Guthrie to open the first Stratford Shakespeare Festival season in a tent.) John Price checked out the Hyannis and Skaneateles operations, as well as Terrell's original Lambertville Music Circus in the summer of 1953.

"These were going concerns, and I learned as much as I could from my flying visits as to how they were set up, how they cast, where they got their tents and chairs and technical equipment like switchboards and lights," he recalled.

Price began to calculate what it would take to raise such a tent in Cleveland. He once claimed to be the type who never worried where the money was going to come from, but a couple of similar ventures had recently gone belly up. "So it was immediately dubbed 'Price's Folly,'" Price said of his own project. It was his wife, Connie, who suggested that he go to see her cousin, Robert H. Bishop III, a lawyer.

Bishop was also a Mather, in fact the son of Connie's namesake, Constance Mather Bishop. He was the last person Price thought would be interested in theatrical ventures; oil wells were much more in his line. Price was also a little leery about taking advantage of his relationship with Bishop, but he figured that at least the lawyer could put him in contact with moneyed people who might be interested in his idea. So he trotted down to Thompson, Hine, and Flory in the National City Bank Building and left a prospectus of his plans with his cousin by marriage.

The lawyer was properly dubious at first. He told Price that it looked more speculative than an oil deal, and he would hesitate to recommend it to his friends. A few days later, however, he called Price back. "I've been thinking about this," he said, "and I think I figured out how we could make a go of it." His use of the plural pronoun started bells ringing in Price's head, just like Sarah Brown in *Guys and Dolls*. "I was thrilled," recalled Price. "I had never even hoped seriously that Bob would want to be involved himself." After grilling Price with a barrage of questions, Bishop came up with a plan.

"He rigged it like an oil deal," Price explained. Rather than the traditional limited-partnership arrangements of most Broadway investments, Bishop opted for a corporate form of organization in which each investor would actually put up only 10 percent of his stake in cash, with promissory notes pledging the remainder. Those notes provided collateral on which the corporation could borrow the money to finish the project. If the venture failed, the investors could deduct the rest of their guarantees against tax liabilities. That loophole was closed by the Supreme Court a few years later, but by that time Musicarnival was off and running.

Both Bishop and Price agreed that the enterprise should have sufficient capital to go first class. Price remembered some advice he had once received from former Cleveland City Manager William R. Hopkins. "He said 'Johnny, just remember this,' in his good Welsh accent, he said, 'Clevelanders will pay anything for the best, but they will not give you a wooden nickel for the second best.'" Bishop was also interested in quality, such as a tent that wouldn't get blown away with the first stiff wind, tying up production and undermining public confidence. He aimed for an initial capitalization of $120,000, nearly double that of most previous musical tents.

According to Price, Bishop was able to raise the entire sum in a single afternoon on the telephone. Much of it came from the family: Bishop himself, his mother, Connie's father, and Price. Significant shares came from such civic and business leaders as Kenyon Bolton, Courtney Brown, Frank Griesinger, David S. Ingalls, Alfred M. Rankin, and Frank Taplin. "They wanted it [Musicarnival] to be a popular cultural asset, just like the orchestra and the art museum," said Price of his board. Rankin was on the board of the Cleveland Orchestra's Musical Arts Association, while Taplin was president of the Cleveland Institute of Music. Smaller investments came from Emma Price, Connie, and publicist Marsh Samuel.

With an eye on publicity, Price prompted Bishop to pitch the venture to former Clevelander Bob Hope. The comedian didn't need much persuasion to join the group. As William McDermott, dean of the city's drama critics, speculated in the *Cleveland Plain Dealer*, "I don't know whether Hope's interest in the enterprise is prompted by local pride, a wish to promote theatrical art, a desire to make a little money, or the fact that the scene of operations is adjacent to a racetrack."

Actually, the Thistledown site was not chosen to attract Hope's dollars or even to hedge the odds of theatrical fortune with the possibility of track winnings. Unwilling to leave such a vital factor as location to chance, Price sought the expert advice of Howard Whipple Green, who had been tracking population trends in Cleveland for a quarter-century. He had served as director of the Bureau of Statistics and Research of the Cuyahoga County Public Health Association, supervised the 1930 Federal Census in Cleveland, and organized and directed the Real Property Inventory of Metropolitan Cleveland. As Price's luck would have it, Green's daughter Patty Ann had been a fellow member of the Cleveland Heights Players in high school.

Green got out his census charts and maps and, waiving the handsome consulting fee he might have commanded, reviewed the demographic profile of Greater Cleveland with Price. "I had all the communities, all the villages, all the suburbs, how much growth they had in the last five years, the last ten years, the last twenty years, which way is the growth in Cleveland taking place, income, where are the high income groups, where are the college graduates in the community," Price recalled. He drew a circle on the map wherein he might reach the majority of the county's culturally inclined inhabitants, and the center of the circle happened to fall in Warrensville Heights. And the most suitable plot of available land in Warrensville Heights happened to be adjacent to Thistledown racetrack.

Articles of incorporation for Musicarnival were filed in the state capital on March 1, 1954. Price's personal preference for a name had been Midway Carnival, thinking of his location (a bit optimistically, perhaps) as a convenient drive from Akron as well as Cleveland. "I was persuaded by cooler heads that a carnival midway was not exactly the term to attract an up-scale clientele, and so finally, Musicarnival was decided upon," said Price. At least he got to keep the carnival imagery, which he felt conveyed the sense of fun he wanted his theater to foster.

But the carnival image didn't sound appealing at first to the intended host suburb. Although the Thistledown racetrack itself was located in the village of North Randall, the land it proposed to lease to Musicarnival fell within the boundaries of the bedroom community of Warrensville Heights. "The plan smacks more of a circus than a theater-in-the-round for musical comedy and light opera production," commented Mayor William J. Racek, who also cited concerns over traffic congestion. "The consensus among school board members is that this enterprise will add to safety hazards and will not be an educational asset for the children of the community," chimed in the president of the Warrensville Heights school board.

"I think it would have been easier to have opened a bordello," Price later reflected on his political woes. Fortunately he had Bishop argue his case before the suburb's zoning board and city council. Musicarnival would bring culture to Warrensville Heights, offsetting its past image as a racetrack center. Perhaps more persuasively, Bishop also pointed out that the theater would add from $4,500 to $9,000 to the city's annual tax revenue. Supporters outnumbered opponents two to one at the zoning hearing, which resulted in a positive recommendation for a permit to city council. The following night, council gave the proposal its unanimous approval, requiring the promoters to pay for any extra traffic signals or police needed and reserving the right to terminate the three-year permit with cause.

Outside of Warrensville Heights, Musicarnival received much more positive press. "Musicarnival will be the first new, major theatrical development in Greater Cleveland in recent years," observed Omar Ranney in the *Cleveland Press*. "The idea is that one sees musical comedies and operettas done arena-style—in 'the round'—under a canvas tent," he explained. "Seats, tent, outside banners, ticket wagons, concession wagons, etc., provide a circus or carnival atmosphere, while the emphasis in the shows inside is on comedy and melody." He might have added, had he only known, that this would also be the city's last commercial, for-profit, legitimate theatrical venture.

Now all John Price needed was a tent and a company. For the tent he turned to Cleveland architect Robert A. Little who, as Bishop did with the financial arrangements, came up with something a little different. All the eastern tent theaters had copied the design of traditional tents. Viewed from above, they were, in Price's words, "wiener-shaped"; from the horizon they suggested the outline of a Bactrian camel. Large half-poles supported the two humps, with quarter poles propping up the sagging center section. The stage inside was actually oval-shaped rather than round, and the profusion of poles partially blocked some views.

Robert Little, known in local architectural circles for a group of modern homes he designed in Pepper Pike, gave himself a crash course in arena-style theaters. His completed plan for Musicarnival called for a large, perfectly circular tent anchored not by a center pole but by a unique "teepee" of three ten-inch steel poles. From a bale ring at the top would stretch thirty-six steel cables, which would bear the canvas covering. "We discovered that more safety as well as better visibility could be secured by having the canvas supported by a steel tripod and stretched under cables," explained Little, adding, "the tent has been developed in such a manner that it can neither blow up or down."

Before Little could proceed to realize his blueprint, however, the last farm on Warrensville Center Road had to be cleared from the site. When Musicarnival took up its lease from Thistledown, Mary and Matthias Grimm had been living for more than six decades in a ninety-year-old farmhouse without running water or central heat. Mary, sixty-five years old, got her water from a hand pump in the kitchen and still churned her own butter. Matt, her sixty-one-year-old brother, raised vegetables and kept a couple of cows. Musicarnival spared their house and slate-roofed barn for conversion to dressing rooms, rest rooms, storage, and offices.

Late in May a steam shovel and bulldozer moved in to excavate the bowl for the arena. Concrete foundations were then poured in concentric circles for the fourteen rows of seats. The only major snag came when Price attempted to move the barn from the south side of the grounds to his theater site. It had to be done by the opening of the racing season, because Thistledown wanted the land for parking. In order to save a few hundred dollars, Price chose the lowest bidder, who then proved unable to get the barn shored up properly to keep it from collapsing. Another lesson: Price had to have the barn burned and then turned to Little for an emergency backup plan. The architect responded with a cement blockhouse topped with a "butterfly roof" for dressing rooms, ticket offices, and other ancillary functions.

As a crane raised Musicarnival's big top for the opening season, actress Carolyn Adair was on hand for the photo-op. A one-time resident of Lakewood, Adair was cast in the leading role of Laurie for the inaugural production of *Oklahoma!* John L. Price Jr. Musicarnival Archives, Cleveland Public Library.

Meanwhile, Little's steel tripod was raised and ready to receive its canvas covering. Early in June the $15,000 tent, comprising 4,500 yards of flameproof fabric, arrived in nine sections from the Central Canvas Company of Kansas City. The blue "roof" was raised with the aid of a fifty-foot crane and a mile and a half of Manila rope. When in place, it measured 140 feet in diameter. Alternating side panels of orange and white completed the festive color scheme.

Inside, $7,000 worth of canvas deck chairs were arranged on the circular terraces surrounding the perfectly round stage. None was farther than forty-four feet from the edge of the stage. Outside, an oval drive was laid approaching the tent for valet parking, with general parking for five hundred cars available in an unpaved lot. It wasn't ideal, but it was more than Cain Park ever had.

"I believe it is unquestionably the largest, best equipped, safest, most comfortable, best-vision Summer Theatre yet built," Little said of his completed project. "I will leave its beauty, or lack thereof, to others to evaluate," he added. "I am personally as satisfied with it as any work we've ever done." The boss was certainly satisfied with its looks, with Price calling it "one of the most beautiful" tents ever made. Compared with the somewhat ungainly contours of the other tents, Musicarnival had an undeniably crisp elegance, one that might well have inspired a more sophisticated product.

By this time Price had also assembled his initial production team. Bob Bishop, now intrigued by the possibilities of show business, agreed to serve as president and brought his law firm of Thompson, Hine, and Flory on board as legal representatives. Investors Al Rankin and Frank Griesinger were respectively secretary and treasurer. Michael Weinberg was named business manager, and Maggie Wheeler from the Cleveland Play House became Musicarnival's box-office treasurer.

Price himself filled the dual role of vice president and producer. Looking for some general guidance on the latter function, he found the managers of similar ventures reluctant to share their professional secrets. "Everyone was afraid I was going to build a theater across the street from them," he explained. "I tell them I'm from Cleveland, show them my driver's license, my credit cards, all this Cleveland stuff. You're from Cleveland, yeah, but you're going to move to New York, aren't you?"

Once again Price's network of theatrical connections came to the rescue. His Bostonian father-in-law, Philip Mather, had a dilettantish interest in theater, dating from his days in Cleveland. After moving to Massachusetts, he had become a principal angel of the Dennis Playhouse on Cape Cod, assuming its mortgage during the

Depression to save it from foreclosure. The Dennis Playhouse also happened to enjoy the services of a crack auditor named Eddie Lutz, and Price thus gained entree to some of the inside information he needed on organizational and budgetary matters. Soon the theatrical accounting firm of Lutz and Carr was hired as a consultant by Musicarnival, as was Herman Krawitz, who had helped establish a couple of New England tent theaters.

When it came time to hire a stage director, Price didn't need any consultants. He turned to his old classmate and Cain Park colleague, William C. Boehm. Besides his Cain Park credits, Boehm had worked with Price in the minimusicals at the Alpine Village and sung operetta locally with the Civic Light Opera League and the Cleveland 500. National exposure came with the *Chicago Theatre of the Air* over the Mutual radio network. Boehm had worked in the round as an actor, if not yet as director, and in a pinch he could do double duty as a romantic tenor.

For his musical director Price hired a veteran of Serge Diaghilev's legendary Ballet Russe de Monte Carlo. Boris Kogan had since conducted for the Detroit Civic Light Opera Association and the Melody Fair tent in Danbury, Connecticut, as well as the Music Circus in Hyannis. He would initially lead an orchestra of nine members at Musicarnival, with an organ filling in for the woodwind parts. Concertmaster would be Ben Silverberg, former violinist and second concertmaster for the Cleveland Orchestra.

Broadway veteran James R. Nygren joined the team as choreographer. He had danced with the Metropolitan Opera Company and done choreography for several television shows. His wife, Ana Barlow, who was from Brecksville, would partner with her husband as principal female dancer.

Set designer Don Ingalls fell ill before the season began, but fortunately Price had a capable assistant on hand to take over. That was his wife, Connie, who had majored in drama at Bennington College in Vermont and had done graduate work at Boston's Leland Powers School of the Theater. Before coming to Cleveland and marrying John Price, she had gained further experience in Massachu-

John Price gathered veterans of Musicarnival's first season for a picture on the tent's fifth anniversary. Seated (left to right) are Eddie Murray, program seller; Connie Price, scene designer; John Price, producer; Emma Moskopp Price, organizer of the Women's Committee; and Boris Kogan, musical director. In the back row are Bill Boehm, actor and director; Sammy Kleinman, electrician; Jack Pollack, violinist; Margaret Wheeler Stevens, box-office treasurer; Ben Silverberg, concertmaster; Joyce McConnell, dancer; and Donn Driver, actor and director. John L. Price Jr. Musicarnival Archives, Cleveland Public Library.

setts with the Dedham Playhouse and Richard Aldrich's Cape Playhouse. She would continue as Musicarnival's principal scene designer for the first few seasons.

By June, Price had also announced his repertoire for the inaugural season. He would open his theater with a ten-day run of Rodgers and Hammerstein's *Oklahoma!* followed by mostly weeklong runs of *The New Moon, Roberta, The Student Prince, Finian's Rainbow, Show Boat, Annie Get Your Gun, Carousel,* and *The Desert Song*. "The plays are the cream of our contemporary music show theater, which in my judgment, is the best in the world," commented William McDermott in the *Plain Dealer*. "They will be acted by professionals and the reasonable presumption is that they will be good." Advance

MUSICARNIVAL

AT THISTLEDOWN RACE TRACK · WARRENSVILLE HEIGHTS

PRODUCER: JOHN L. PRICE, JR.   PRESIDENT: ROBERT H. BISHOP III

By Special Arrangement with
RODGERS & HAMMERSTEIN

Presents

"OKLAHOMA!"

Music by Richard Rodgers
Book and Lyrics by Oscar Hammerstein 2nd
Based on the play "Green Grow the Lilacs" by Lynn Riggs
Originally Produced by Theatre Guild
Staged by William C. Boehm
Musical and Choral Direction by Boris Kogan
Choreography and Musical Numbers Staged by James R. Nygren
Set Designs by Don Ingalls

CAST OF CHARACTERS

(In order of their appearance)

Aunt Eller Murphy	Mary Marlo
Curly McClain	Ridge Bond
Laurie Williams	Carolyn Adair
Fred Denham	Gordon Bray
Ike Skidmore	Stanley Propper
Will Parker	Donn Driver
Jud Fry	Rowan Tudor
Ado Annie Carnes	Judy Rawlings
Ali Hakim (The Peddler Man)	Harold Gary
Gertie Cummings	Thelma Dalpe
Old Man Carnes	Frank S. Stevens
Cord Elam	Frank Borgman
Aggie	Joyce McConnell
Curly (in the Dream Ballet)	James Nygren
Laurie (in the Dream Ballet)	Anne Barlow
Jud (in the Dream Ballet)	Maurice Nystrom

Farmers...Keith Mackey, Sam Collura, Laurence Stith, Jr.
Cowboys...................Byron Brice, Dave Hladik
Girls........Carol Selleck, Evelyn Haddad, Joy LaForge
          Charlotte Fairchild, Nanci Hall, Gloria Paul
Ballet........Ruth Kuzub, Sandra Sane, Charles Morrell

Stage veteran Mary Marlo headed the cast of Musicarnival's opening production of *Oklahoma!* followed by Ridge Bond, who sang the first notes heard from its circular stage. This was the first of some ninety "snake programs," measuring approximately 6 x 18 inches, distributed to patrons during the production years. John L. Price Jr. Musicarnival Archives, Cleveland Public Library.

All was in readiness for Musicarnival's debut on June 24, 1954, as cars dropped off passengers from the approach drive, and expectant theatergoers lined up outside architect Bob Little's cement auxiliary wing to enter the graceful round tent. It was a summer scene repeated for twenty-two seasons. John L. Price Jr. Musicarnival Archives, Cleveland Public Library.

tickets went on sale at Halle's downtown department store and were reported to be moving briskly at prices ranging from $1.25 to a weekend top of $3.50.

While he wanted a strictly Equity company, Price was also determined to cast as much as possible from local talent. "I always cast here first, then went to New York to fill in, which didn't make New York too happy," he explained. For *Oklahoma!* he recruited most of his principals from the road companies that had been crisscrossing the nation for a decade. Ridge Bond had notched more than two thousand performances as Curly, while Mary Marlo had played Aunt Eller so often, including fourteen months in London, that her own personality had become subsumed into that of the down-to-earth homesteader. In Carolyn Adair, Price found both a seasoned Laurie and a local girl. A former Lakewoodite, Adair had sung at the Alpine Village before touring the United States and Australia in an *Oklahoma!* company. She had also done three seasons of theater-in-the-round at Toronto's Melody Fair.

Since the tent wasn't quite ready for them, Bill Boehm and Boris Kogan began rehearsing their cast at Shaker Junior High School. Price was generally stuck in Bob Little's concrete blockhouse back on the Musicarnival grounds, trying to attend to a thousand last-minute details at a makeshift desk, consisting of a sheet of plywood bridging a pair of two-drawer filing cabinets. Finally he couldn't resist sneaking off to the school to peek in at the rehearsals. As he walked down the hall towards the auditorium, the company happened to burst into the show's rousing title song. Price didn't need to hear any more. Wheeling around, he headed back to more mundane problems of lighting and plumbing. "You're doin' fine, Oklahoma! Oklahoma, O.K.!"

Some of the pressure was taken off the producer's hands by his mother, Emma Price. Just as she had done at Cain Park twenty years earlier, Emma was aiding in the formation of a Warrensville Heights Women's Committee for Musicarnival. Where three months ago the suburb had been trying to keep Musicarnival out as an undesirable neighbor, Mrs. Price now had its wives and mothers working in the theater's support. Their first project was the preparation of a buffet supper for the company before the dress rehearsal.

Somehow it all came together by Friday evening, June 25, 1954. Arthur Spaeth of the *Cleveland News* confessed to some shock at "the efficiency with which an able parking crew stashed away the motor cavalcade that streamed into the grounds right up to curtain." As for the grounds, they reminded *Cleveland Press* society columnist Winsor French of "the shed at Tanglewood in the Berkshires, except that the countryside is less manicured and, I think, more beautiful." Once inside, *Plain Dealer* critic Glenn C. Pullen recorded "murmurs of astonishment when the audience saw the terraced bowl-shaped auditorium, with three huge steel poles supporting acres of mottled blue canvas."

In the inaugural Musicarnival program book, John L. Price Jr. addressed "the People of Northern Ohio," noting, "Although the idea of presenting shows 'in-the-round' in tents has already been highly successful in some other parts of the country, this will mark the first time that an arena theater has been housed in a circular tent. . . . We hope you will be pleased with this new addition to the cultural and civic life of the area and that you'll find yourself spending many happy evenings at Musicarnival."

Offstage, Price handed out corsages in the dressing rooms to the female members of the company. It was 8:45 P.M. before he made his way to the stage to face a nearly full house of close to 1,700 faces. "Good evening, neighbors!" he began, as he would for more than two thousand performances to come. Then he added a line tailored specifically for that special night: "And welcome to the fulfillment of a dream!"

2

Production Years I:
From *Oklahoma!* to Opera

I
t began just as the modern American musical itself had begun eleven years earlier: an elderly woman seated alone on an uncluttered stage, working (like the shade of the recently dispossessed Mary Grimm) at her churn to some soft, sprightly rhythms in the strings. From the outer edge of the tent came a clear baritone solo,

"There's a bright, golden haze on the meadow . . ."

and Ridge Bond as Curly sauntered down the aisle to serenade Mary Marlo as Aunt Eller in the farmyard.

It was a beautiful mornin' for Musicarnival as it opened on June 25, 1954, with Rodgers and Hammerstein's classic *Oklahoma!* This was the musical that had revolutionized the form when it arrived on Broadway in 1943. Radio, recordings, and road companies had spread its sunny message across the nation since then, including eight stops for a total of ten weeks at the Hanna Theatre in downtown Cleveland. The last visit had been less than two years earlier in 1952. Musicarnival, however, was giving Cleveland its first local, professional production of the show.

Oklahoma!—the show that revolutionized the Broadway musical—proved to be a propitious choice as Musicarnival's inaugural production in 1954. Its exuberant dance numbers captivated critics and audiences alike. John L. Price Jr. Musicarnival Archives, Cleveland Public Library.

There wasn't much of a plot to speak of, and what it boiled down to was a question of whether pretty young Laurie was going to go to a frontier social with the genial cowboy, Curly, or the sullen hired hand, Jud Fry. No matter; characters and story line (thin though it was) were thoroughly believable, and all of the songs flowed naturally from characters and plot. Between the opening "Oh, What a Beautiful Morning" and the concluding title song were half a dozen more standards, including "The Surrey with the Fringe on Top," "People Will Say We're in Love," and "Out of My Dreams."

John Price and company did the show full justice. "A new kind of theater has come to Cleveland, and it deserves a lusty Oklahoma 'Yipee-eye-ay,'" exulted Omar Ranney in the *Cleveland Press.* "What the audience saw was a Broadway-caliber production from the stars to the bit players and members of the ensemble and ballet." For Arthur Spaeth of the *Cleveland News,* Musicarnival's staging of the folk opera came off "as fresh as a daisy and professional in the most flattering sense of the word."

Bob Little's tent theater also received its share of raves. "I have visited the major ones, and completely aside from any civic pride, I can say that Musicarnival is now the finest of all of them," observed Ranney. "To begin with, its completely circular tent, the first of its kind, is far better than any of the other music circus tents." Praising the theater's "rare feeling of warm, informal intimacy," Glenn C. Pullen in the *Plain Dealer* stated, "Nobody could ever complain about a lack of visibility or a poor seat." About the only disagreement voiced came over the tent's acoustics. Spaeth marveled that the singers could be heard "without benefit of mike. It is refreshing and wonderful to hear singers sing au natural again. . . . The memorable songs ring clear and clean to the farthest seats—I tested it out." Ranney obviously heard the show from a different vantage point, complaining that the female singers in particular were in need of "a little more amplification."

All in all, it must have been the most memorable week of John Price's life. On hand to capture it on film for a feature spread on summer theaters for *Life* magazine was famed photographer Gordon Parks. When the article appeared later that summer (August 2, 1954), a Musicarnival picture appeared at the top of the story. One Parks shot that didn't make the final cut showed Price tossing cigars out to the audience before a performance of *Oklahoma!* He was announcing the birth of his third child, Philip Mather Price, on June 30. It remained for *Variety,* the show business weekly, to summarize Musicarnival's debut in its inimitable shorthand: "OKLA. BOFF $30,000 AT CLEVE. CARNIVAL TENT."

For his second show, Price dipped into his Cain Park memory bag for the old-fashioned Sigmund Romberg operetta, *The New Moon.* Ridge Bond played the romantic lead opposite Rosemary Kuhlmann. "I have seen it several times and I am not sure as to what the story is about, except that it represents a kind of romantic nonsense which is used as a thread on which to string some musical pearls," wrote William McDermott in the *Plain Dealer.* "The scene is New Orleans of the late 18th century and the story is not worth exploring."

Still, the dean of Cleveland's theater critics had finally shown up at Musicarnival despite initial misgivings. "It is a long way from my usual scene of operations, and I supposed the ride might be tedious and the tent hot," McDermott explained before rendering his verdict: "It was not uncomfortably warm. It was pleasant and delightful. So was the show." Arthur Spaeth of the *News* singled out such Romberg melodies as "Stouthearted Men" and "Lover Come Back to Me" for amply redeeming the show's "dusty book." One line, however, according to cast member Stu Levin, struck the opening night audience as particularly relevant as the chorus sang "Oh, dainty wisp of thistledown" against the aroma of the neighboring horse barns.

When Connie Price experienced labor pains during the opening run of *Oklahoma!* her husband John told her she couldn't have the baby until she finished the set designs for *Roberta.* She did, and the Jerome Kern musical comedy opened on schedule as Musicarnival's third show. Musical theater veteran Jack Cassidy headed the cast, seconded by Patricia Ruhl, a Cleveland Institute of Music graduate. McDermott called their efforts "a delight to hear and a pleasure to behold." To the *Press*'s Ranney, however, viewing the musical's two acts was "almost like being at two different shows. In the first part . . . they lacked about everything it takes to bring a musical comedy to life." Then things picked up, and Ranney singled out two secondary players for their comedic efforts. Joan Kibrig "walked off with the show" as Schwarenka, said Ranney, and Donn Driver "injected a good deal of comedy" into a role originated on Broadway by a young Bob Hope. Both would play larger parts in Musicarnival's future.

The pros and cons of in-the-round staging were brought out by Musicarnival's production of Romberg's classic operetta, *The Student Prince.* Bill Boehm not only directed but also assumed the lead role of Prince Karl Franz. "Old Heidelberg does not seem the same when stripped of its colorful scenery by modern 'in-the-round' stagecraft,"

A major talent that emerged in Musicarnival's first season was that of comic actor Donn Driver. He was featured in the role of the leprechaun Og in *Finian's Rainbow* and is seen here with some of the children in the production. John L. Price Jr. Musicarnival Archives, Cleveland Public Library.

protested Pullen in the *Plain Dealer*. "This skeletonizing technique, despite handsome period costumes and pleasant singing, seems to rob the operetta of its glamorized Graustarkian traditions which made it so popular for exactly 30 years." In the *News,* Noel Francis saw the glass as half full rather than half empty. "The fact is that something new has been added," he observed. "This critic is of the belief that the result is far more charming than the old, though 'faithful reproductions' of Heidelberg atmosphere."

Newer musicals seemed to fare better under Musicarnival's stripped-down style. *Finian's Rainbow* was next, and Ranney pronounced it the theater's best effort to date. "Something akin to magic has taken place at Musicarnival," he told readers of the *Press*, "for with only a week's rehearsal time the company has put together a show that in sustained entertainment rivals anything produced by the Broadway touring companies of 'Finian's Rainbow.'" Though he "hardly [knew] where to begin" in distributing kudos to an outstanding cast, the critic singled out Driver for playing the difficult role of Og the leprechaun to "comic perfection."

After the opening week-and-a-half of *Oklahoma!* most of the remainder of Musicarnival's schedule had consisted of one-week stands. Price was following the advice of "New York sources," who had assured him that a single week was all the traffic would bear in the hinterlands. "After one show [had opened], we would have a meeting and discuss next week's show," recalls director Bill Boehm. Determined to give his company a mid-season breather, Price ignored the experts and scheduled a single two-week run for the beginning of August. "So we ran *Show Boat* . . . and naturally the second week was better than the first and the boys from New York had egg all over their fat faces," Price observed. "I knew this was a two-week town, dammit, this is my town. I know what she'll do and what she won't do."

Show Boat was a good choice for Musicarnival's two-week experiment. Though more than a quarter-century old, the Jerome Kern and Oscar Hammerstein show had prepared the way for the transition from the older operetta to the modern musical play. Ageless numbers such as "Make Believe," "Can't Help Lovin' That Man," "You Are Love," and, of course, "Ol' Man River" didn't hurt its chances, either. McDermott had seen the original production when it had its tryout in Cleveland's Ohio Theatre prior to its Broadway premiere in 1927. While the Musicarnival revival necessarily lacked much of the spectacle of the Ziegfeld original, he thought it compensated for the loss by allowing the audience to concentrate on the "glorious tunes" and the "touching, sentimental story." An able cast was headed by John Tyers as Ravenal, Paula Stewart as Magnolia, and Rosemary Kuhlmann as Julie, but McDermott saved his highest praise for another actor. "William C. Smith sings and acts the role of Joe as well as I have ever seen it done," he wrote, "and I have seen both Jules Bledsoe and Paul Robeson in the part."

Three bit-players also came in for special notice in that production. John Price finally got into the show, making his acting debut on the Musicarnival stage as a World's Fair barker (type-casting, some might say) in the opening scene of the second act. His four-year-old daughter, Diana, then made her first appearance on any stage as the Ravenals' daughter, Kim. And in the show's final scene, Cain Park veteran Emma Moskopp Price as the Old Lady on the Levee gave the Price family three generations in one show. Noel Francis closed his review in the *News* with "a special round of applause" for Diana. "You can show this to producer papa and demand a raise," he wrote. Fortunately, the critic wasn't there the night Diana "went up" on her lines. She remembers just "looking blankly at the audience" until John Tyers whispered the line under his breath. "Daddy, can I go with you?" she finally repeated. "Then he forgot his own line, and I had to feed it back to him."

It was back to a one-week stand for Musicarnival's next production, Irving Berlin's *Annie Get Your Gun.* Ridge Bond returned to the fold to play Frank Butler, but the show belonged to Susan Johnson as the titular heroine, sharpshooter Annie Oakley. "She is just right for the part," said Ranney in the *Press.* Making the most out of Musicarnival's circular layout, director Boehm had Annie perform her precision shooting from the back of a motorcycle roaring around the outside perimeter of the tent.

Demand for tickets for the following show was so great that Price extended the run for Rodgers and Hammerstein's *Carousel* to two weeks even before opening night. As one of the most serious of the new musicals, it presented Musicarnival with perhaps its biggest challenge of the season. Baritone John Shafer was brought in from the Hollywood Bowl to portray Billy Bigelow, with Broadway's Arlyne Frank as his Julie Jordan. Carolyn Adair returned to play Carrie Pepperidge, and Bill Boehm took the stage again as her suitor, fisherman Enoch Snow. "That is a favorite song in musical theater for tenors," says Boehm of "When the Children Are Asleep," his duet with Adair. "In some ways, the performance at Musicarnival seems to be better than the productions I have seen in New York and on

Bill Boehm, Musicarnival's first director, was also one of its leading tenors. In *Carousel* he assumed one of his favorite roles, fisherman Enoch Snow, opposite the Carrie Pipperidge of Carolyn Adair. John L. Price Jr. Musicarnival Archives, Cleveland Public Library.

the road," said McDermott in the *Plain Dealer*. "The singing is of a high degree of excellence." Audiences obviously agreed, as they gave Musicarnival its record crowd of the season for *Carousel*. With the addition of folding chairs in the rear, 1,894 took in one performance.

As his inaugural season neared its end, John Price was clearly on a roll. He closed with another Cain Park standby, Romberg's *The Desert Song*. Headed by John Shafer as the Red Shadow, the cast was now full of familiar faces: Bill Boehm, Frank Stevens, Donn Driver, and Carolyn Adair appeared in major parts, while Keith Mackey stepped up from the ensemble to a speaking role. An old Cleveland favorite, radio announcer Wayne Mack, appeared as Ali Ben Ali. The mellifluous baritone was a veteran with Boehm of the operetta seasons of the former Cleveland 500 company. "Probably because I know Mack, I found it difficult to believe his having a harem with a thousand girls, all of whom were to be bathed and 'filled with wine,'" observed Ranney in the *Press*, "But the theater is a place of many wonders." Ranney couldn't resist adding that Mack's shoes squeaked. Pullen gave credit to Donn Driver for "chopping out many of the show's dreadful old puns" and "lightening up the action with inventive new bits of comic business" in his portrayal of Benjamin Kidd. Neither squeaky shoes nor old puns hurt the box office, as *The Desert Song* was good for another extended two-week run.

With the final performance of *The Desert Song* on September 19, John Price could finally catch his breath and assess his first season as a producer. As of its final week, Musicarnival had drawn ninety thousand patrons, an average of over one thousand per performance. With gross receipts passing the $200,000 mark, there had even been a small profit, unusual for a startup season. Bishop's investors never had to back up their promissory notes. One prominent backer, however, was bought out by mutual consent. Bishop and Price had needed the approval of all investors for major expenses, and the peripatetic Bob Hope was almost impossible to locate at most times. "There was no ill will or rancor or anything like that," commented Price. "It just didn't work out from a practical point of view."

Connie and John Price spent the fall storing Musicarnival property in the old Grimm farmhouse, which still stood on the grounds. The canvas tent was taken down for the winter and stored with the chairs in the auxiliary building, but the steel tripod remained standing as symbolic evidence that the theater would be back. Price spent his last winter as Mr. Weather-Eye (another Cain Park alumnus, Frank Cover, replaced him), quitting the newscast the following March to become a full-time producer.

According to *Variety*, the show-tent movement was on the upswing, with at least five new "teepees" scheduled to join the ten already in operation in 1955. "On the basis of last year's highly competent performance, it would seem that we can put our trust in Musicarnival to people its in-the-round stage wisely and well," observed Arthur Spaeth in the *Cleveland News*. "I am told that Johnny Price, the producer of the Musicarnival shows, and his associates had little trouble in engaging Broadway performers for the current season," revealed McDermott in the *Plain Dealer*. "They were anxious to come, not so much because they needed the money but because they had heard that conditions were especially good from the actors' viewpoint. That means the theater itself, the audiences, the management and the dressing-rooms."

John Price wasn't content to rest on his laurels, as he undertook an ambitious program of improvements on the Musicarnival grounds. A second entrance drive and unloading point was added, and both drives were widened and blacktopped. East of the theater a picnic ground was opened that could be used by patrons (who were advised to book reservations) before the shows. By March, Price was ready to announce a schedule of six shows for 1955: *Kiss Me, Kate; South Pacific; Die Fledermaus; Brigadoon; Wish You Were Here;* and *Guys and Dolls*. All would be given minimum two-week runs, with *Kiss Me, Kate* booked for two-and-a-half weeks and *South Pacific* for three weeks.

Price had secured the first summer-stock rights to *South Pacific*, the Rodgers and Hammerstein smash hit from 1949 that had even eclipsed the pair's *Oklahoma!* It came with a stiff guarantee of $2,000 a week and a potentially knotty string attached: the casting was subject to the final approval of Rodgers and Hammerstein. Susan Johnson, Musicarnival's Annie of the previous season's *Annie Get Your Gun*, reportedly was nixed by the New York office in favor of Mimi Kelly, who had understudied the Nellie Forbush of Mary Martin on Broadway. She also happened to be the daughter of actor Paul Kelly. For the Ezio Pinza role of Emile de Becque, Musicarnival would have John Shafer from last summer's *Carousel* and *The Desert Song*. Lee Krieger, who would play Luther Billis, and Stanley Grover, who would be Lieutenant Joe Cable, were both veterans of *South Pacific* road companies.

Scene changing was a show in itself at Musicarnival, as apprentices bringing props on the stage dodged exiting actors and audience members sitting on the aisles. "This musical has the busiest palm trees since the last hurricane swept the South Pacific," noted one critic of a *South Pacific* production. John L. Price Jr. Musicarnival Archives, Cleveland Public Library.

What generated the most local excitement, however, was the engagement of Juanita Hall for the pivotal role of Bloody Mary, the Tonkinese native who motivates much of the show's action and comedy. She had been one of the first hired for the original cast, Rodgers himself describing her as "high spirited, graceful, mischievous, proud, a gloriously gifted voice projected with all the skills of one who knew exactly how to take over a song and make it hers." As Clevelanders who listened to the original cast album were well aware, Hall indeed owned her two numbers in *South Pacific*, "Bali Ha'i" and "Happy Talk." Short (five-foot-one) and stocky, she was built something like a spark-plug and performed a similar function on a stage.

South Pacific opened in the round on June 27 to rave reviews in the Cleveland papers. "I count it the best play and the best production I have seen there," said McDermott in the *Plain Dealer*. Ranney of the *Press* concurred that it was Musicarnival's best effort to date. "You almost feel that the Rodgers-Hammerstein musical was written especially for arena-style production," he added. None of the cast was found wanting, but Hall in particular was deemed equal to her billing. "When Miss Hall made her first entrance, the effect was the same as adding a hundred volts to the electric current," observed Ranney. McDermott termed her "a tower of strength in the role of Bloody Mary," whose assurance rubbed off on the rest of the cast. Even the stage crew got its share of praise for its quick scene changes. "This musical has the busiest palm trees since the last hurricane swept the South Pacific," remarked Ranney.

About the only discordant note came from Cleveland's Catholic weekly, the *Universe Bulletin*. Reviewer Timothy A. Murnane gave the show in general high marks as "first class entertainment featuring splendid music, evocative settings and fine characterizations, plus a couple of side swipes at racism." What he took issue with was the plot's side themes, especially the romantic subplot involving Cable and Bloody Mary's daughter Liat. "There's no recognition that their action is evil: it's pictured as perfectly normal, even beautiful," protested Murnane. In a flash of premature political correctness, the critic also chastised the play's sailors and Seabees for teaching Bloody Mary such Americanisms as "stingy bastards." Moralizing that "such debasement of natives is not funny," Murnane labeled *South Pacific* "objectionable in part."

It would appear that the *Universe Bulletin*'s objections had the often-unintended effect of bringing out the curious to see things for themselves. Even three weeks weren't enough to fill the demand, as Price decided to hold over *South Pacific* for an unprecedented—and never surpassed—fourth week. He needed a new Nellie, Billis, and Cable, but fortunately his Bloody Mary remained available. Originally Hall had signed on for a singing engagement at Kornman's Back Room on Short Vincent Street; she managed to get a release for the extra week at Musicarnival by agreeing to go downtown nightly following *South Pacific* and do two shows after midnight for Kornman's.

The only recalcitrance she displayed came when the nightclub crowd requested her rendition of "Bali Ha'i." "Please, anything but that," begged off Hall, who estimated she had done the number more than two thousand times. Director Boehm recalls that on the final night of *South Pacific* one of Hall's admirers drove up to Musicarnival with a sedan full of champagne. "Juanita stood there pouring champagne for the cast, the apprentices—for everyone," says Boehm. "She was a great gal."

Not far behind *South Pacific* in popularity during the second season were the Musicarnival productions of *Wish You Were Here* and *Guys and Dolls*. It was an Ohio premiere for the former, a 1952 effort by Harold Rome that had never toured, no doubt because few road houses could satisfy the set requirement of a real swimming pool on stage. Based on Arthur Kober's play *Having Wonderful Time*, the musical dealt with nothing more challenging than the romantic problems of staff and guests at a summer resort in the Catskills. Undaunted by the pool challenge, Price had assured critics at the beginning of the season that "there'll be wimmin swimmin'." His solution was simply to line the Musicarnival orchestra pit with plastic and fill it with thirty tons of water. Boris Kogan and the band headed for the heights at the back of the tent for the duration of the run.

"Who cared about the plot, or lack of it, when there was such good singing and dancing? And diving?" asked reviewer Oscar Smith in the *Akron Beacon Journal*. Among those taking the plunge were Musicarnival president Bob Bishop and publicity director Marsh Samuel, making cameo appearances in Gay Nineties bathing gear. The "swimmin' wimmin" included Terry Rosen, wife of Cleveland Indians slugger Al Rosen. Spectators in the first two rows behind the "pool" were issued plastic slickers to ward off the excessive splashing. "We didn't want to create too much disturbance—it was just the novelty of seeing that water," says director Boehm. (Nevertheless, when the show was revived four years later, a drenched woman was seen leaving the fourth row and squishing up towards the exit, mad as a wet hen.)

Our Short Vincent Reporter
Reviews Musicarnivals Guys'n' Dolls...

Cartoonist Bill Roberts saw a natural affinity between Musicarnival's production of *Guys and Dolls* and the racing fans of the neighboring Thistledown racetrack. His "Week's Wash" was a popular front-page feature in the Saturday *Press.
Cleveland Press,* September 3, 1955.

Guys and Dolls had been one of John Price's favorite shows since
the days he had pirated it for Herman Pirchner's Alpine Village. That
created a potential complication when Price went to New York to
negotiate for rights with the show's agent, Alan Whitehead. He was
uneasily aware of Whitehead's "fishy eye" during their first encounter.

When he returned to finalize the deal, Whitehead gave expression to his doubts: "Someone in Cleveland was stealing our show—do you know who it was?" As humbly as he could, Price acknowledged that he was the culprit. "*You* were the son of a bitch!" erupted the incredulous agent. Business was business, however, and Price got the rights, even if he didn't get the discount he had the chutzpah to ask for.

Musicarnival gave the show everything it had. "Fireplugs, street corner rubbish containers, magazine stands (where the Daily Racing Form was sold), and various tables for the customers of the snappy Hot Box Cafe were rushed on and off the stage in an almost miraculous succession of 16 scenes," noted Ranney in the *Press*. Donn Driver and Joan Kibrig appeared as Nathan Detroit and Miss Adelaide, while John Price appropriated the brief part of his favorite Runyanesque character, Rusty Charlie. In the opening "Fugue for Tinhorns," when he sang, "I got the horse right here!" he pointed up to the edge of the tent, where the spot picked up a genuine thoroughbred just inside the flaps. "Of course, working near Thistledown, we had no problem getting a horse," says Bill Boehm.

They had no problem getting audiences either. For the second time that summer Price held the show over an extra week, giving *Guys and Dolls* a three-week run. His biggest reward probably came in the form of a "Dear John My Pal" wire from the show's creator, Frank Loesser. "Jimmy McHugh just returned from Cleveland and raved about the great performances that you and all of the dolls and guys are doing," said Loesser. "After all the performance is the thing. On behalf of your entire cast and yourself will you please accept my sincerest thanks." Any past indiscretions were obviously forgiven, and Price even invested in a later Loesser show on Broadway. It was *Greenwillow,* the composer's first flop.

At the end of its second season, Musicarnival posted a gross take of $245,000 for the fourteen-and-a-half weeks. *South Pacific* headed the list with $84,000 over four weeks, followed by *Guys and Dolls* ($55,000 for three weeks) and *Wish You Were Here* ($38,000 in two weeks). Attendance totaled 130,000 patrons, a 40 percent increase over the first year. "These figures place Musicarnival in the uppermost ranks of the country's rapidly increasing tent enterprises," asserted Price in a *Plain Dealer* ad.

Price's production team by this time had solved most of the problems of arena staging. While most regular theatergoers may already have seen *Oklahoma!* noted McDermott prior to the initial Musicarnival production, "I doubt that any of them have seen the play staged in the arena manner, where the spectators view the action from four sides, as they do in a circus. It must give a well-known play a certain novelty and freshness and it must create problems for the director and the actors." A few weeks later, however, the *Plain Dealer* critic returned to the subject to observe that, in a historical context, Musicarnival's staging wasn't as novel as modern audiences might think.

McDermott cited the Roman arena as a direct precedent, as well as the in-the-half-round stagings of the Greek and Elizabethan theaters. "There was no curtain in the Elizabethan theater," noted McDermott, nor was there much in the way of realistic scenery. "Scenery was a fairly new conception in the history of the theater," he wrote. "It was formerly left to the imagination of the audience." Or as John Price puts it, "I'd tell the audience, 'If you don't believe in fairies, what the hell are you doing here?'"

Cleveland audiences—at least the more sophisticated segment thereof—were not complete strangers to arena-type staging. In 1949 the Cleveland Play House, then acknowledged as America's foremost regional theater, opened a new theater in a converted church featuring a thrust, or apron, stage. Anticipating Canada's Stratford Festival by three years, it attracted national attention for its ability to stage Shakespeare in a reasonable approximation of the Elizabethan manner. That same year the interracial Karamu Theatre included an intimate arena stage in its new complex on Quincy Avenue. It was frequently employed for musical productions, particularly the avant-garde operas for which Karamu became noted.

Most of the staging at Musicarnival was in the hands of Bill Boehm. "This exciting new form brings out the best," he had told Price on the basis of his acting gig at the Finger Lakes tent. "The audience is all around—how do you reach them?" Now he had to answer his own question, and he had no contacts at Karamu to consult. "We didn't have time to meet with other people," he recalls. "We just went ahead and did it."

Boehm could draw on his own tent show experience for some solutions. One of the earliest problems solved by "Sinjun" Terrell concerned the positioning of the chorus vis-à-vis a soloist. On a conventional proscenium stage the answer is obvious: place the soloist in front of the chorus. There being no rear on an arena stage, however, Terrell had to figure out how to keep the soloist in view of the entire audience. The solution? Simply have the chorus kneel or sit around the standing soloist. Performers also learned to go to the edge of the stage for big numbers and then turn around, thus facing nearly three-quarters of the audience. One traditional staging problem actually solved itself in arena staging. Characters could speak directly to one another without worrying about facing the audience; nobody could be upstaged in the round.

"More fluidity was required in acting and directing in the round," says Boehm. "You can't have a standing picture too long. You can't stay in one area too long, you had to move around." Because of what he refers to as "that invisible situation"—always having part of the audience behind an actor's back—Boehm insisted that actors had to put more into their performances. Hall told McDermott that she tried to "act with her back" for the benefit of those behind her. "She means that dejection, or anxiety, joy or pleasure can be shown by the posture of the body even if you cannot see the face of the player," the critic explained.

Arena staging presented both "a challenge and an opportunity," in McDermott's words. "You always had to have a solution, like when you had to create a swimming pool for *Wish You Were Here*," says Boehm. For a revival of *Show Boat*, one of Boehm's successors made innovative use of the tent's half-aisles, which bisected the wider rear portions of the theater's nine wedge-shaped sections. For the show-within-a-show in the first act, they became theater boxes for the characters viewing the play on the main stage. Then, as described

Needing a swimming pool for its 1955 production of *Wish You Were Here,* set designers simply flooded the Musicarnival orchestra pit. Smart producers provided plastic slickers to keep the front-row audience dry. John L. Price Jr. Musicarnival Archives, Cleveland Public Library.

by Harlowe Hoyt in the *Plain Dealer,* "In the World's Fair interlude, the boxes hold a collection of banners and freaks with a bearded lady, a dog-faced boy, a snake charmer, and all the sideshow retinue plus a barker to expound their virtues." To find a solution for *Peter Pan* that same season, Musicarnival called in stage technician Peter Foy, who had devised the show's flying effects for Mary Martin and some two thousand performances. Foy managed to adapt his stage machinery to tent proportions, floating not only five characters in the play but young volunteers from the audience afterwards. He even managed to hoist a two-hundred-pound reporter named Don Robertson for a feature in the *Cleveland News.*

Stage directors weren't the only ones confronted with new challenges. Musical director Boris Kogan had to devise his own bag of tricks to reach singers who were facing in the opposite direction. Sometimes he would "telegraph" his cues through singers facing him, who would pass on the cue through a nod to the others. Singers not facing Kogan also learned to count beats to know how long to hold a note. To direct singers stationed in the back of the tent or in the half-aisles, Kogan employed a small flashlight in his left hand, while conducting the orchestra with his right.

Connie Price and later set designers also came up with their own solutions. In lieu of backdrops, Bob Little's steel tripod could be adorned with cardboard cutouts suggesting the play's locale. A circular valance high above the stage might be similarly decorated. It served to mask the lights and some minimal set effects (e.g., the ceiling of Jud's smokehouse in *Oklahoma!*), which might be flown in for certain scenes just as in a proscenium stage. A liberal use of props also compensated for the lack of scenery. For *The Music Man,* set designer Edward Graczyk II came up with a versatile prop that served variously as a set of railroad tracks, the top of a rolling cart, and an upright fence.

With no curtain or wings to work behind, scene and prop changing, as well as entrances and exits, sometimes became a show in itself. "The players make their entrances and exits down and up the darkened aisles of the theater," observed McDermott about that first season, "and the swish of skirts as they make their way creates a breeze which is only slightly unhoneyed by your fear that they may fall down before they get where they are going." Ranney claimed that odds were being taken in the front row during *Guys and Dolls* that "before the evening was over someone would break a leg." The only casualty, however, came when a crew member dropped and then tripped over a piano stool he was carrying up an aisle. During another production, a chaise lounge sped past Ranney so fast and close that he speculated on the possibility of being "carted onto the stage by mistake." A young Keith Joseph, viewing *I Do! I Do!* much later, reported having had a baby carriage dropped on him. Aisle spectators who crossed their legs were liable on occasion to have their shoes removed and their feet tickled by an impish actor waiting in the darkness for his entrance.

So arena staging not only put the actors in the middle of the audience but also sometimes put the audience in the center of the action. "At Musicarnival, I experienced an odd change of status," reported Arthur Spaeth about *West Side Story.* "I ceased to be a member of an audience. Caught in the neo-primitive world of the Jets and Puerto Rican immigrant Sharks; the love-at-first-sight romance of Latin lass and Nordic lover, and the fear, hate and violence that explode to litter the street with the dead, I became an actor in the drama. The helpless onlooker, aware of the impending tragedy but unable to stop it."

Some problems of tent-theater staging were never completely overcome. Rain was one of them. While not entirely at the mercy of the elements, as at Cain Park, the audience at Musicarnival was exposed to the pitter-patter of raindrops on the canvas roof. It was like "beating on a drum," recalls Boehm, who stopped *South Pacific* one evening when rain drowned out Hall's rendition of "Happy Talk." Dimming the stage lights, the director snuck down to whisper that they would reprise the song after the rain. "She said the song was ruined, but when the rain stopped she did it again and got a terrific hand," relates Boehm. Trying to play through a downpour could be more stressful for a cast than waiting it out, as Stan Anderson noted in a *Show Boat* review. "It must be utterly frightful when there is a huge noise on the canvas, . . . when water seeps through the tent and when an audience gets restive along with the weather," he wrote in the *Press.* It was generally better to stop, as they did the following year in a rain delay during *The King and I.* Boris Kogan led the audience in communal singing of such oldies as "Pack Up Your Troubles in Your Old Kit Bag," and a couple of dancers came up with an impromptu routine. When action resumed an hour later, the audience was in a forgiving mood.

Rain or (moon)shine, the acoustics of circular staging remained another nagging problem. "I come from a generation that when God gave you a voice, you used it," says Price, who opened Musicarnival with no amplification system. As noted earlier, the tent's acoustics received mixed reviews. Though no auditor was more than fifty feet from the stage, half the audience at any moment was behind the singer rather than in front. "You had to speak loud—if they can't hear, they won't understand the story," says Boehm. "It was amazing how well it did work." Nonetheless, Price eventually had to give in and consider some form of amplification. "We had to experiment a lot because arena sound is trickier," says Price, who explains that Musicarnival came up with a system that enhanced sound behind the actors while letting the audience in front hear the natural voice. It was installed in 1960 by Jack McCormack, a versatile public-relations man, who solved the problem with the use of fourteen microphones and seventy-two speakers.

Apart from any technical problems, some shows intrinsically seemed to be better suited to arena production than others. McDermott noted at the very outset of Musicarnival, "Some types of plays are not suitable to this kind of production." Generally, critics seemed to think that the older operettas suffered by comparison with the modern, post-*Oklahoma!* musical plays. Price divided his inaugural season almost evenly between the two styles, with operetta represented by three Romberg works, *The New Moon, The Student Prince,* and *The Desert Song.* To this trio might be added two Jerome Kern works, which more or less combined features of the older and newer styles—*Roberta* and *Show Boat.* On the whole, critics (and presumably audiences) seemed to miss the romantic scenic trappings of these shows—the old Heidelberg of *The Student Prince,* the exotic Morocco of *The Desert Song,* and the Mississippi River steamboat of *Show Boat.*

All four of the newer musicals of that first season proved to be solid hits: Rodgers and Hammerstein's *Oklahoma!* and *Carousel,* Irving Berlin's *Annie Get Your Gun,* and Vernon Duke and E. Y. Harburg's *Finian's Rainbow.* One of the strongest characteristics of the new musical play was its more realistic plot, which suggests that these works had stronger legs to support them on a nearly bare stage. Operetta went into a noticeable decline over the next few seasons at Musicarnival, as the star of the musical play shot into the ascendant.

Of course, a simpler, equally valid explanation for the rising popularity of the musical play was the freshness of the newer form. Musicarnival made its bow in the middle of the golden age of the Broadway musical. The twelve years between 1943 and 1954 saw the premieres of the four Rodgers and Hammerstein classics: *Oklahoma! Carousel, South Pacific,* and *The King and I.* They also witnessed the late masterpieces of Irving Berlin and Cole Porter, *Annie Get Your Gun* and *Kiss Me, Kate,* respectively. Frank Loesser made his mark with *Guys and Dolls,* while Alan Jay Lerner and Frederick Loewe contributed *Brigadoon* and *Paint Your Wagon.* Other mileposts of the period included Harold Arlen's *Bloomer Girl,* Jule Styne's *Gentlemen Prefer Blondes,* and Leonard Bernstein's *Wonderful Town.* Barely six weeks before the opening of Musicarnival, the new songwriting team of Richard Adler and Jerry Ross burst upon the Broadway scene with *The Pajama Game.*

Most of these shows hadn't been seen in northern Ohio since they toured at the Hanna, and John Price grabbed them for Musicarnival as fast as they became available. He had the first stock rights for *Oklahoma!* in 1954 and for *South Pacific* the following year. In 1956 he got *The King and I,* last of the "Big Four" of Rodgers and Hammerstein. He then revived *South Pacific* in 1957, *Oklahoma!* and *Carousel* in 1958, and *The King and I* in 1959. *Guys and Dolls, Annie Get Your Gun,* and *Wish You Were Here* were also revived during the first six years. Having offered the Ohio premiere of *Wish You Were Here,* Price performed the same honors for another non-touring show, *Plain and Fancy,* in 1956. In 1957 he presented both *Can-Can* and *Silk Stockings* by Cole Porter, as well as *The Pajama Game* and *Damn Yankees* by Adler and Ross. Other shows getting early exposure at Musicarnival included *Wonderful Town* and *Bells Are Ringing.*

Nationwide, the tents were going through new musicals faster than Broadway could turn them out. All nineteen of the theater tents performed *The Pajama Game* in 1957, its initial summer release year. Paul Mooney of the *Cleveland Press* went to Buffalo's Niagara Melody Fair in 1960 to preview *Redhead,* scheduled to be seen at Musicarnival later that season. Without Gwen Verdon, around whom the Broadway original had been built, he deemed it "second rate" stuff. The only other new show to hit the tents that summer was *West Side Story,* as Broadway held onto such hits as *My Fair Lady, The Music Man,* and *The Sound of Music.* For the first time in its seven-year history, noted Mooney, there would be no Rodgers and Hammerstein show at Musicarnival. "'One Enchanted Evening' loses its magic easily if brought back too often," he observed. "So back to Friml, Herbert, and Romberg," concluded Mooney in a reference to the older operettas. "At least they wrote melodies."

Characteristically, John Price came up with a different idea. One of the great passions of his life, right alongside Shakespeare, was grand opera. He had even appeared onstage with the Metropolitan Opera Company as a supernumerary, or "spear carrier," during the New York company's annual spring visits to Cleveland's Public Auditorium. As usual, he burned to share his enthusiasm with others. Price would sometimes refer to Musicarnival as his "cultural kindergarten," his daughter Diana observes. "He wanted people to have so much fun that they would go on to Shakespeare and grand opera." While he never tried Shakespeare in the tent (beyond such Bard-derived musicals as *Kiss Me, Kate,* at any rate), opera wasn't that far from what he was doing. Questioned once about the danger of running out of fresh material, Price answered, "Well, that's one of the reasons why our venture in opera is so important. There's a whole repertory there that's untouched."

The venture began as early as Musicarnival's second season with a production of Johann Strauss Jr.'s *Die Fledermaus,* an ambiguous work straddling the border between opera and operetta. Price used a successful Broadway version known as *Rosalinda.* It called for operatic voices, however, so Price went to New York to hold auditions. Among those answering the call was a young soprano with flaming red hair and vocal pipes to match. "She came in with [agent] Henry Reese and sang the 'Czárdás,'" recalls Price with a beatific smile. "After three notes we didn't have to hear any more, but we let her sing the whole goddam thing." She got the job. It was the then-unknown Beverly Sills.

Originally scheduled for a two-week run, *Die Fledermaus* was bumped back to one week because Price held over the phenomenally successful *South Pacific*. "That gave us two weeks of rehearsal, and by God, it was one of the best things we did," he remarks by way of compensation. "She would come to rehearsals looking like the cleaning lady—very down-to-earth," recalls Bill Boehm of Sills. "When she stepped on that stage, she was no cleaning lady—she was radiant, in her beautiful red hair. She was the epitome of elegance."

Critics happily agreed. "Possessed of a delightful lyric quality, Miss Sills' soprano voice is destined, along with her personal charm, to carry her high among the concert artists of this era," Lyle McKay wrote presciently in the *Erie Dispatch*. "She reaches for a high D as gracefully as she flicks her fan or raises her champagne glass." In the *Cleveland Press*, Ranney approvingly described the soprano's physical qualifications for the "Strip Duet" she sang with her maid while changing into costume onstage for Prince Orlofsky's ball. "Even the notes she sings are round," he marveled.

Sills later remembered Musicarnival as "a first class operation all the way." Invited with other cast members to a pool party on the Hunting Valley estate of Bob Bishop, she began dating the Musicarnival president and called him "my first real beau." That fall, however, Sills finally made an impression at the New York City Opera. When the company visited Cleveland on tour, she attended a party at the Cleveland Press Club, where she met another potential beau. He was Peter Greenough, president of the Press Club and an editor at the *Plain Dealer*. Though he was in the process of going through an acrimonious divorce, she began seeing him, and it soon developed into a serious relationship.

So perhaps John Price had something more going for him than just his first-class operation when he signed Beverly Sills for two operas in the following summer of 1956. The first was another crossover work, Franz Lehár's *The Merry Widow*. Sills played the title role, supported by Mace Barrett, Lloyd Thomas Leech, and Stephanie Augustine. Though he gave the soprano high marks for her rendition of "Vilia," Ranney found the production on the whole somewhat deficient in romantic atmosphere. "Where there should have been soft lighting, as in the fantasy of moonlight, the lights shone harshly on Miss Sills," complained the *Press* critic. "What she brought forth was entirely by virtue of a lovely and well-disciplined voice."

Carmen was a different story. This was no hybrid work, but Price used an English version by Virginia Card and George Huston that returned to composer Georges Bizet's original concept of spoken dialogue between the set pieces. Sills had never sung the title role before, though she had appeared in the secondary part of Micaëla. Her mother Shirley, who always made Beverly's costumes, simply recycled her old Micaëla costume into a Carmen outfit. Price didn't skimp on a supporting cast for his Carmen, with Lloyd Thomas Leech as Don José and New York City Opera bass-baritone Norman Treigle as the toreador, Escamilo. "I just wanted to have fun with the role," recalled Sills, who came up with special "business" with Treigle. "I'd like to be a friend of yours," said the toreador to Carmen, who replied, "You already have enough friends." "Yes," said Escamilo, focusing on Carmen's bosom, "but I want to be a *very* good friend." According to Sills, "The audience loved it, as did Norman."

And as also did Jack Warfel of the *Cleveland Press,* who wrote, "For wide-scale production this is possibly the best packaged 'Carmen' yet devised." Noel Francis noted in the *Cleveland News* that if Sills could maintain the pace (which she did), it would mark the first time in Cleveland history that an opera had been given with the same star for fourteen straight performances. "Early in the performance she establishes her importance to the action," he commented. "When she is not on stage the audience can feel the letdown." McDermott was only slightly less enthusiastic in the *Plain Dealer,* praising her "pure, true and warmly musical" singing but judging her interpretation of the role to be somewhat on the light side. Actually the role was far more suited for a mezzo than her lyric soprano—it was her first and last Carmen. It was also her first, but far from last, operatic duet with Norman Treigle.

That fall Beverly Sills married Peter Greenough and moved into his twenty-five-room mansion in Cleveland's posh lakefront sub-

Taking a break outside the tent during *Carmen* rehearsals were director Michael Pollock, Beverly Sills, Norman Treigle, Lloyd Thomas Leech, and Stephanie Augustine. It marked the first time that Sills and Treigle worked together, beginning an artistic collaboration resumed years later in several momentous productions at the New York City Opera. John L. Price Jr. Musicarnival Archives, Cleveland Public Library.

urb of Bratenahl. Among her neighbors were William McDermott and John Price. From there she could commute the following summer to Musicarnival, where Price was planning a production of Giacomo Puccini's *Tosca* around her. Tenor William Olvis would sing the role of Cavaradossi, while the villainous Scarpia would be portrayed by William Chapman of the New York City Opera, who had played the King the previous summer in Musicarnival's *The King and I*. Michael Pollock, who had staged last year's *Carmen*, would be in charge again for *Tosca*. "This is our aim—not to ram opera down the public's throat, but to show that it need not be long hair or for the precious few," John Price wrote beforehand in the local publication *Fine . . . Music.* "We are out to prove that opera belongs on the stage—not in the museum or the conservatory. . . . We merely wish to be instrumental in returning it where it belongs—to the general public—as a rare and wonderful form of theater magic."

Price hoped to realize his aim with a new English translation by John Gutman, assistant manager of the Metropolitan Opera. Gutman updated the plot by transferring it from Rome during the Napoleonic Wars to an unnamed East European police state of the contemporary Cold War. In the second act Scarpia listened to Tosca's performance of a Victory Cantata over the radio, then let her hear the screams of the tortured Cavaradossi over his intercom. And since Tosca could hardly jump from a castle parapet on Musicarnival's circular stage, she committed suicide in the last act by stabbing herself with the same letter opener she had used earlier on Scarpia. To accompany Puccini's lush score, Boris Kogan stretched Musicarnival's cramped orchestra pit to the limit with seventeen players, including six strings.

Musicarnival's *Tosca* garnered national and even international notice. There were pictures and brief reviews in *Time* and *Opera News.* Sills displayed "a true dramatic flair and a voice to match," local critic Frank Hruby wrote for *Musical America,* adding that Chapman's "acting was just about perfect and he sang to all parts of the surrounding audience with equal ease and authority." Hruby reported that the opera played to nearly full houses, averaging 1,700 audience members, for seven nights. "Originality is this outfit's middle name," declared Lucien Price in the *Boston Daily Globe.* "To take the formal starch out of opera while still leaving it 'grand,' . . . and do it in full artistic stature both as music and drama, while proving that it can pay its own way, these are the high hurdles and watch Musicarnival clear them with a clean pair of heels." Finally, there came what sounded like a rave from *France-Soir* in Paris: "*Les spectateurs sont ravis.*"

But no one raved with more gusto than the producer. "Some day Mr. Bing and [the Metropolitan Opera] Co. can come out here to find out how to make good opera come ALIVE on the stage," John Price stated in a memo to his company. "It's the most difficult thing in the world to do—and you did it!"

Of course, it didn't come entirely without mishaps. A malfunctioning blood capsule turned one performance of *Tosca* into a Grand Guignol spectacle. When stabbed by Tosca in Act Two, Chapman as

Scarpia inadvertently held the capsule the wrong way; instead of spreading across his white shirtfront, the "blood" sprayed all over Sills instead. Chapman collapsed on the stage more in suppressed laughter than simulated pain, and the audience was on the verge of breaking up as well. The only one not about to laugh was Sills, who was determined to avoid the disintegration of her carefully sustained characterization. With innate diva temperament, she sobered up Chapman with a swift kick, unmindful of the fact that he was already down. Miraculously, that also seemed to quiet the audience, perhaps fearful themselves of the wrath of Tosca's fury. There was an extra-long intermission before the last act, however, while they wiped the blood off the soprano. Determined not to let it happen again, Price says that his "backstage wizards" concocted a disappearing blood. Unfortunately their specs proved to be slightly faulty. "One night it disappeared too soon—it was like the Immaculate Conception!"

For his next operatic act Price originally planned to follow up *Tosca* with Puccini's *La Boheme*. Just before the 1958 summer season, however, Beverly Sills scored a sensational triumph in the New York City Opera production of a recent American work. Price quickly scratched Puccini from his schedule and prepared to give the Midwest premiere of *The Ballad of Baby Doe*. Based on historical personages from Colorado mining days, it told how Baby Doe, the "miners' sweetheart," stole the heart of Silver King Horace Tabor, endured ostracism by Tabor's first wife and Denver society, but remained true to Tabor long after the collapse of his fortunes. Sills would recreate her success in the title role, seconded by two other members of the New York cast, Walter Cassel as Tabor and Cleveland Institute of Music graduate Beatrice Krebs as Baby Doe's mother. Two familiar Cleveland faces, Bill Boehm and Wayne Mack, landed the prestigious roles of President Chester Arthur and presidential candidate William Jennings Bryan, respectively. Cameo appearances as Tabor and Baby Doe's young daughters were made by Sills's new stepdaughters, Nancy and Lindley Greenough.

Composer Douglas Moore, quondam director of music for the Cleveland Museum of Art, made an appearance for the opening

The crowning production of Musicarnival's "operatic venture" was the Midwest premiere of Douglas Moore's *The Ballad of Baby Doe* in 1958. Cleveland radio personality Wayne Mack made a memorable appearance as William Jennings Bryan (at right) in the election scene. Beverly Sills appeared as Baby Doe, here seated under the mine entrance with her two daughters, who were played by the soprano's own stepdaughters. John L. Price Jr. Musicarnival Archives, Cleveland Public Library.

night on September 8, 1958. His opera received glowing reviews, with Harlowe Hoyt of the *Plain Dealer* calling it the "Most noteworthy of all productions at Musicarnival's tent since its beginning." Hoyt also thought that Sills had surpassed her previous tent efforts: "She was never in better voice than yesterday.... She had made Baby Doe her own and I can imagine no other singer equaling her in the part." In the *Press*, Frank Hruby singled out Walter Cassel for the evening's honors "with his full baritone, extraordinary diction and expert characterization." Moore's score won the praises of Oscar Smith in the *Akron Beacon Journal,* while Ethel Boros in the *Cleveland News* saved some laurels for conductor Boris Kogan, who somehow managed to squeeze twenty musicians into his pit for this production.

Sills might have begun to think Musicarnival's stage was jinxed, as *The Ballad of Baby Doe* didn't pass without another accident. This time it was a capricious stage elevator, which was supposed to take Baby Doe slowly down into her husband's old mine at the very end of the opera. "On that last note, she was holding it going down into the mine," remembers Price, when suddenly he heard the note break. That wasn't all that broke. The elevator jerked and took her to the bottom so fast that Sills broke her nose, but she gamely came up smiling for the curtain calls. "She was a good scout," says Price.

Unfortunately, Musicarnival's *Baby Doe* joined that group of productions labeled as critical successes but box office failures. Attendance fell off after opening night, and Price lost nearly $15,000. Once he had dreamed of a mini-season-within-a-season of two or three operas and even of commissioning a new work from Gian Carlo Menotti. Now he added up the figures from his operatic venture:

1958	*Baby Doe*	$27,936.09	
		13,161.23	
		14,477.86	loss
1957	*Tosca*	$24,095.03	
		18,786.10	
		5,308.93	loss
1956	*Carmen*	$45,150.87	
		30,439.35	
		14,711.52	loss
1955	*Fledermaus*	$26,773.97	
		22,509.50	
		4,264.47	[loss]

and the bottom line was a total loss of $39,059.78. As Price had said of opera, "Dammit, it has to pay its own way." He still talked of doing

La Boheme and Offenbach's *The Tales of Hoffmann,* and later revived *The Merry Widow* and *Die Fledermaus,* but for all intents and purposes, the operatic experiment was over.

Though his backers had nervously suggested a temporary suspension of opera for the 1959 season, Price refused to hold them responsible for the decision. Writing to an old wartime acquaintance in England, he bitterly groused, "I was so sore at the stupid public, I decided to cease and desist casting pearls before swine." He described the glories of *The Ballad of Baby Doe.* "It is real Americana, a part of our history, and I presented the finest production of it that has ever been done anywhere. Nobody came. So to hell with the damned peasants! Let them come to see the warmed-over Broadway slop they seem to like so much!" It was 1959, and the Musicarnival box office had just been broken by another slice of Americana. "The thing that broke our record (which broke my heart)," he says, "was *Li'l Abner.*"

Opera seemed to be the only battle John Price couldn't win. During what he would later refer to as "the glory years," not even nature could stop Musicarnival. There was the 1956 production of *Kismet,* for example, in which the Wazir was "drowned" in a well at the end by being pushed down one of the stage trapdoors. As Price tells it, "One night [actor] Michael Kermoyan comes up with a wild-eyed look and says 'Jesus Christ, there's skunks down there!'" Price had installed pipes under the stage to keep it warm for the dancers, which made it an ideal nesting place for "a whole goddam family of skunks."

When ushers reported having seen them scavenging for popcorn and other tidbits in the back rows during a show, Price knew he couldn't leave them in peace. If a spectator happened to feel one brush against her legs and let out a shriek, Musicarnival could have a theater panic on its hands. Should a skunk panic in return, there could be an even bigger stink. "I had to get out the twenty-two and go after them," says Price, no Nimrod by nature. "I got myself sort of loaded up at first, so all I did was shoot a couple of holes in the tent." At that point wiser counsels prevailed, and Price called in the Animal Protective League.

Tattered but unbowed, Musicarnival survived the tornado of 1958 with its revolutionary tripod still standing. While awaiting the arrival of a new tent from Florida, John Price continued with his schedule of shows—under the stars. John L. Price Jr. Musicarnival Archives, Cleveland Public Library.

A few seasons later, nature issued a much stiffer challenge. During a performance of *The Desert Song* in late August, Musicarnival's tent flaps began snapping ominously. "Oh, it's a desert breeze," ad-libbed one of the actors on stage. That was a slight understatement, as the Weather Bureau reported tornado-force winds between seventy to more than a hundred miles per hour sweeping in over Lake Erie from the northwest and slashing across Cuyahoga County. Three were killed on the West Side as a water tower crashed through five floors of an aluminum factory. At Musicarnival, the winds opened two-dozen rips up to forty feet long in the canvas tent, exposing the audience to a drenching rain. They remained calm, however, as staff members directed those on the windward side to the stage for greater safety. Above them, Bob Little's steel tripod stood firm against the gale.

"Thank you, Robert A. Little!" was the headline on an ad Price placed three days later in the Cleveland newspapers. "Mr. Little, you would have been PROUD to see how your 'Queen of the Big Tops' took that Sunday punch," read the copy. "She flapped her shredded cloth in defiance, and she protected like a mother eagle the multitudinous brood beneath her. NOT ONE PERSON WAS INJURED!" Though called a "tent theater," Price explained to reporters that Musicarnival was in reality "a permanent building of steel cables and concrete with a canvas roof."

In effect Musicarnival had merely had its roof blown off—or half off, at least. Under normal wear and tear and weathering, it had to be replaced every few years anyway, and a new $11,000 replacement had already been on order from Sarasota, Florida. Price was told it would be ready in about ten days. Until then, he had the tattered remains of the old tent removed and announced that Musicarnival would complete the run of *The Desert Song* and open its next offering of *Gypsy* under the stars. As Price put it in his testimonial to Bob Little (with no apologies for another "overdose" of exclamation points), Musicarnival's "scarred and faded pennant is still up there flying—proclaiming boldly according to the ancient tradition of Shakespeare's day, that THE SHOW WILL GO ON!!!"

3

Production Years II: Cinderella Story

R
ichard Rodgers couldn't make it, but two thousand Clevelanders showed up for Musicarnival's proudest moment. It was the world stage premiere on June 5, 1961, of Rodgers and Hammerstein's *Cinderella*. "As we explained it is impossible for me to leave New York at this time," the composer had telegraphed John Price three days earlier. "However I can express my deep gratitude to you for doing Cinderella and I do wish you an enormous success. All my thanks and kindest regards."

True, more than one-hundred-million Americans had seen the original television special starring Julie Andrews on CBS in 1957. But no one had ever seen that version live on stage prior to the opening at Musicarnival. It came about through the intersection of two separate flights of fancy. In his never-ending search for new material, John Price had been urging Richard Rodgers to let him have some of the Rodgers and Hart shows rewritten and updated for straw hat revivals. He told the composer that he had just the man for the job in his multitalented young director, Don Driver.

Rodgers, who had recently lost his second collaborator, Oscar Hammerstein II, had a different though not necessarily incompatible

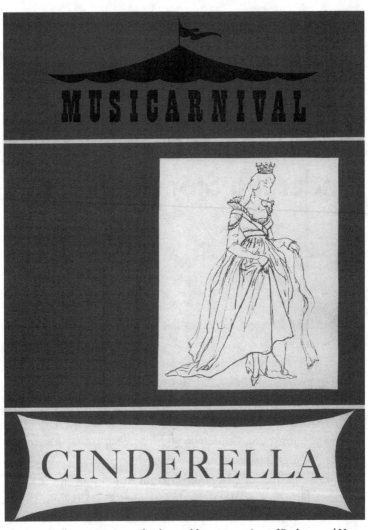

Musicarnival's program cover for the world stage premiere of Rodgers and Hammerstein's *Cinderella* featured Paul Rodgers's costume design for the title character. John L. Price Jr. Musicarnival Archives, Cleveland Public Library.

agenda. He and Hammerstein had talked about reviving *Cinderella* for the stage before the lyricist's death in 1960. Now he sent for Don Driver, not to discuss Rodgers and Hart but to size him up for Rodgers and Hammerstein's *Cinderella*. When he returned, Driver was the new, if not quite the full, partner of Richard Rodgers.

So John Price became the producer of a Rodgers and Hammerstein premiere, even if for a second-hand show. Nevertheless, only one other Rodgers and Hammerstein show had ever opened outside the traditional East Coast tryout towns of New Haven and Boston. That was *Me and Juliet,* which happened to have its world premiere in Cleveland at the Hanna Theatre (not a particularly auspicious portent, since that musical turned out to be one of the team's rare failures). The Musicarnival premiere would be the equivalent of a New Haven tryout for *Cinderella,* which was slated to play later that summer at the St. Louis Municipal Opera, the Kansas City Starlight Theatre, and the Sacramento Music Circus.

Driver's main assignment was to flesh out a ninety-minute (including commercials) television program into a full evening's stage entertainment. He started by fashioning a new book around the highly regarded musical score of the television original. Some characters were given more rounded personalities, such as the henpecked but philandering king. His biggest innovation, however, came in the characterization of Cinderella's two wicked stepsisters, who were rewritten to be played in drag by male comedians. Native Clevelander Kaye Ballard had portrayed one of the sisters memorably in the television version; obviously, she need not audition for the Driver adaptation.

Some additional songs were needed too, if only for balance. Unconsciously underlining the Cleveland connection, Rodgers and Driver found spots to recycle "Keep It Gay" and "A Very Special Day" from *Me and Juliet.* Rodgers also opened up his trunk of discarded numbers from past shows and came up with the duet "Boys and Girls," originally intended for *Oklahoma!* and now assigned to Cinderella and the Prince. Still feeling he needed a new song for the transvestite stepsisters, Driver showed Rodgers a lyric he had written called "Ladies in Waiting," and Rodgers obliged by providing it with a melody. It may not have seemed like much, but it put Driver in the rarified company of lyricists who supplied words for Rodgers's tunes.

Now it was up to John Price to give the revamped show a production worthy of the reputation of its original creators. "For its premiere performance Musicarnival has given 'Cinderella' all the care and attention usually lavished on a Broadway production," he claimed in the show's program book. It was directed of course by Don Driver. Sets and costumes were designed by Paul Rodgers, who currently headed the technical department at the Cleveland Play House. He responded with castle-like crenellations above the stage, a royal staircase a full theater aisle in length, and sumptuous medieval costumes. As executed by costume supervisor Sheila Pearl, the latter were compared favorably with those of the Lerner and Loewe musical *Camelot*, then reigning on Broadway. Choreographer Duncan Noble also earned plaudits for his period dances and a magical transformation scene.

Price found a strikingly attractive Cinderella in Monte Amundsen, who had extensive experience in opera as well as in musicals. Her prince charming was Broadway- and Hollywood-veteran Tommy Rall, who happened to be her husband in real life. Bill McDonald and Leonard Drum were the two stepsisters, and television actress Dortha Duckworth was the fairy godmother, or "Plume Lady," as she was dubbed in this version. Familiar Musicarnival players included Alfred Dennis as the king, Lucille Benson as the queen, and Lawrence Vincent as the Chamberlain.

On the whole, critics found more to praise in the production than in the show itself. Both Harlowe Hoyt in the *Plain Dealer* and Paul Mooney in the *Press* felt that the first act was a drag, though Mooney thought the second act good enough to redeem the whole, if judiciously cut. His fruitless efforts "to catch a frontal glimpse of Monte Amundsen" also confirmed to the *Press* critic his belief that "theater-in-the-round was a vicious circle for the audience." All he could say for sure was that the actress had a lovely back. Critics also debated the merits of Driver's masculine stepsisters. "Driver expended most of his Rombergian humor on the pair," said Mooney, "and the audience ate it up like two big bags of popcorn." Hoyt compared them to the Three Stooges, then enjoying the first of many revivals in popularity. But while the adults in the audience may have been splitting their guts, Oscar Smith of the *Akron Beacon Journal* failed to hear any childish laughter. Younger spectators, he speculated, were confused by the humorous take on the familiar story. Kids preferred their stepsisters unambiguously wicked.

Cinderella then was something of a bittersweet coup for John Price and Don Driver. Price had had the excitement and prestige of a Rodgers and Hammerstein premiere, though he thought he had been treated shabbily by the Rodgers and Hammerstein organization. "They didn't give us any break at all," he recalls, pointing out that Musicarnival went 50 percent over its usual budget to do the premiere justice. "It opened the season, so we gave it a little extra rehearsal time, spent more money on the set, got a good cast," he explains. "We're breaking our humps to give it a good show, so I got on the phone and asked for a little break on the royalties. Not a cent!" Driver had the credits for the original stage presentation of Rodgers and Hammerstein's *Cinderella,* though his version was seldom used intact in later revivals. However, the 1965 television remake retained the "Boys and Girls" number he and Rodgers had added from the *Oklahoma!* scrapheap, while the male stepsisters survived as late as a 1990s production in Seattle. As for Cinderella and her prince, Monte Amundsen and Tommy Rall eventually headed from a royal court to the divorce court.

Cinderella nonetheless kicked off a banner summer for Musicarnival. "Johnny Price and his companions at Musicarnival are clearly in a sentimental mood and all summer long their tent is going to be washed with nostalgia," observed Winsor French in the *Cleveland Press.* "No social significance for them, thank you, but sheer gaiety and, believe me, we can well use it." Besides *Cinderella* the schedule included five other productions new to Musicarnival: *The Red Mill, Take Me Along, Paint Your Wagon, High Button Shoes,* and *Bloomer Girl.* There would be only two revivals, *Die Fledermaus* and the eternal *South Pacific.* All the shows, old and new, would bear the increasingly strong imprint of Don Driver.

Victor Herbert's 1906 operetta, *The Red Mill,* was a case in point. Driver not only directed a cast including Broadway star Lee Cass and

It was a tough job, but someone had to do it—and Don Driver did it all during Musicarnival's production years, as evidenced in the production of *Paint Your Wagon*. Driver not only directed the show and performed the lead, but he also arranged the choreography. John L. Price Jr. Musicarnival Archives, Cleveland Public Library.

comedian Coley Worth but also undertook updating the show's humor as well. "Driver lets the comedy go wide open in the show, so at times it almost reaches [again!] the Three Stooges level," wrote Mooney in the *Press*. The director was wise enough, however, not to touch such Herbert classics as "Streets of New York," "Moonbeams," "Every Day Is Ladies Day with Me," and "Jeanette and Her Wooden Shoes." "[T]he essence of Herbert comes sailing through on nostalgia-scented melodies," concluded Mooney. "Here again is proof that an old chestnut can be as satisfying as the latest Broadway show, if it is done right."

Though a then-recent Broadway effort, *Take Me Along* also conveyed a strong whiff of nostalgia, as it was based on Eugene O'Neill's

Ah, Wilderness! The great American dramatist's only comedy, it was a coming-of-age tale set in New England at the turn of the twentieth century. Bob ("How Much Is That Doggie in the Window") Merrill provided a capable score for the musical version, making its Cleveland premiere at Musicarnival. Al Dennis and Renee Orin stood out as Uncle Sid and Aunt Lily, roles originated by Jackie Gleason and Eileen Herlie. "There's excitement and diversion in the parade with fire engines, banners and old-time hoopla," noted Hoyt in the *Plain Dealer,* summing it up as "good hot weather entertainment."

High Button Shoes and *Bloomer Girl* continued the season's good-old-days theme. The former was originally a Phil Silvers vehicle, distinguished principally by an entertaining ballet built around Mack Sennett bathing beauties and Keystone Kops. *Bloomer Girl* was a somewhat stronger piece, written in the Americana vein that followed the success of *Oklahoma!* Based very loosely on the historical character of Amelia Bloomer, it touched lightly on the topics of women's rights and slavery. In an about-face from her Cinderella persona, Amundsen was cast as feminist Evalina Applegate. "She projects all over the place and, for my money, her singing voice will do, even in theater in the round," wrote Stan Anderson in the *Press.*

Artistically, the season peaked with *Paint Your Wagon,* in which Don Driver did everything but paint the scenery. "Driver is amazing in his multiple-talent chores at Musicarnival," said Mooney in the *Press.* "Of course, he is to be commended for lively direction [his twenty-fifth directing chore in the tent] and spirited choreography, but from the audience standpoint it is Driver, the performer, who wins its heart." Driver took the leading role of Ben Rumson, a miner who finds gold in California, founds a town, then moves on after the gold runs out. With numbers such as "They Call the Wind Maria," it was the most underrated of the musicals of Alan Lerner and Frederick Loewe (the awful movie version with Lee Marvin and Clint Eastwood didn't help its reputation either). Norma Joseph, Al Dennis, Providence Hollander, and Lawrence Vincent all contributed to an ensemble performance.

As for the revivals, *Die Fledermaus* featured Amundsen and the Metropolitan Opera voices of Paul Franke and Thomas Heyward. "It's our choice as Musicarnival's best production of 1961!" said Jack Darrow in the *Warren Tribune*. Of course, he wrote that before the season finale of *South Pacific*, making its third appearance under the big blue tent. "Audiences go back to hear it again and again," observed Smith in the *Akron Beacon Journal*. "Why do the people love this show?" Because of its believable characters, he responded to his own question. Webb Tilton and Joan Fagan starred as Emile de Becque and Nellie Forbush, but Don Driver also gained notice for his comic turn in one of his favorite roles, the irrepressible Seabee Luther Billis. John Price had to add a Saturday matinee to the one-week engagement to satisfy the demand for seats.

While Don Driver may have been leaving his mark on the artistic product, Price still remained Mr. Musicarnival in the public eye. He maintained that identification with an innate and consummate sense of showmanship. For *The Ballad of Baby Doe*, he had had his playbills printed in silver ink. He had gone even further with *Damn Yankees*, putting out a red, white, and blue playbill headed, "Official Souvenir Score Card: The Damn Yankees vs. The Cleveland Indians." Musical numbers were listed under the heading of "Batting Order," and the cast was presented as the "Line-up for Tonight's Game." Onstage there were even bigger changes. "In its original form 'Damn Yankees' deals with the trials and tribulations of the Washington Senators," Price explained in the program book, "but because of our understandable hometown pride and staunch local loyalties Musicarnival is presenting this delightful saga of our national sport as a tribute to that eminent and beloved ball club, our own Cleveland Indians." That was in 1957, and the ebullient Price had little idea how many decades would pass before the real Indians could be competitive again with the Damn Yankees.

Baseball and showmanship were a natural combination to John Price, who claimed to have studied with "one of the great showmen in the country today." That was Bill Veeck, former owner of the Cleveland Indians and one-time star in *The Man Who Came to Dinner* at the Hanna Theatre. "He's the greatest since Barnum," said Price. "He set every existing attendance record in major league baseball. . . . Be-

John Price, who took former Cleveland Indians owner Bill Veeck as his model for showmanship, substituted the Tribe for the Washington Senators in his 1957 production of *Damn Yankees*. Casting himself as manager (front), he took his fantasy team all the way to the pennant—something few Indians managers have done in reality. John L. Price Jr. Musicarnival Archives, Cleveland Public Library.

cause this man had guts and imagination and vitality even on one leg to do ten times as much in one day as all the other club owners in both leagues would do in a year." Price learned from Veeck not only through personal observation but by hiring Veeck's former publicity man, Marsh Samuel, to work for Musicarnival. "It's like a gambler on a streak of luck, when things are really going like that and you've got ideas, just keep them coming and keep that audience rocking. Don't ever give them a chance to catch their breath."

The Veeck touch was visible in many of Price's stunts. When *Plain Dealer* critic William McDermott whimsically suggested that critics could use a helicopter to commute to summer theaters out in the suburbs, Price's ears perked up. This was the critic who, when kept from the theater by illness, once received a visit from Katharine Cornell and her troupe, who proceeded to perform their latest play in his living room. Price's company was too large to fit into a living room, but one evening a helicopter showed up in Bratenahl to whisk McDermott and his wife to a Musicarnival opening. "Kenny Bolton had a helicopter company for a time," Price explains, in reference to Musicarnival director Kenyon C. Bolton. "I suppose this is the first time in history that a drama reviewer was carried from his home to the doors of a theater," wrote the obviously impressed critic. Veeck's influence might also be seen in Price's hiring of Ed Murray to hawk Musicarnival programs at the entrance to the tent. The seventy-three-year-old born salesman had started as a "candy butcher" at the old Cleveland Theater on St. Clair Avenue at age eight and later disposed of half a million programs at Cleveland's Great Lakes Exposition.

Even in the off-season, Price never lost an opportunity to promote Musicarnival. Community groups could count on him to bring his slides and give an entertaining talk on his theater. "Sometimes it can get a little ridiculous," he admitted, "like one time I went out to make a speech and [it] ended up there were three girls there." Still, he went, often wearing a Musicarnival tee shirt under his white shirt and tie. "At seminars he would rip open his shirt and say 'Promotion! It's all about promotion!'" recalls his daughter, Diana. Another instance indelibly fixed in her memory came when her father boarded an airplane for Florida and woke up in Havana, courtesy of a hijacker. Interviewed for a local television station upon his return, he explained that he had slept through the whole thing because "I was up so late last night booking a contract with Robert Goulet and Carol Lawrence for the week of September 6 through 11 at Musicarnival. The phone number is 663–8400." And that's how it aired, number and all.

To Price, the key to Veeck's success was "the personal touch. That guy was always in the stands. He was always out on the banquet circuit." And so John Price was always on the Musicarnival stage every evening to personally welcome the audience with his "Good evening, neighbors." "John would always make those great bounding entrances for his pre-show talk, which always ended with a joke, 'Please, no smoking in our fireproof tent,'" recalls dancer Frank Baloga. In between the "Good evening" and the "no smoking," Price would extol the virtues of not only his own show but those of other theaters around town. "Unselfishness such as yours is not unique in theater . . . but it is not in overabundance, either," once wrote Don Bianchi, founder of the alternative Dobama Theatre, thanking Price for promotional support. Chagrin Valley Little Theatre was another frequent beneficiary of Price's precurtain promos. If the Indians were playing during a Musicarnival performance, Price was also likely to reappear before the second act to let the audience in on the score.

Price carried the personal touch beyond the call of duty by following the audience out to the parking lot to bid them good night. This came about not as a result of premeditated calculation, but as an inspired, impromptu gesture. It began after a performance of *Show Boat* the first season, during a heavy downpour of rain that showed no sign of letting up. As some of the braver souls dashed into the deluge towards the parking lot, the bulk of the audience hung back, grumbling darkly in the tent. "The people were so disgusted and wet and miserable that I figured someone from Musicarnival was going to have to get wet too, just so the customers wouldn't feel so bad by comparison," remembered Price. As no one else seemed to be volunteering, he elected himself.

Still in his *Show Boat* costume of a carnival barker, Price sloshed out to the unpaved lot and began waving his cane at the departing cars and shouting, "Thanks for coming, folks!" As he continued there, dodging puddles in the rain, the sleeves of his bright barker's jacket began shrinking upward towards his elbows. The brim of his straw boater became detached from its crown and dropped soggily around his neck like a collar. "People said, 'Who is this village idiot!' but I guess they liked it," remarked Price. When they began complaining that they missed seeing him following subsequent shows, he figured he'd better make it a Musicarnival tradition, rain or no. Even when suffering from laryngitis, he went out there with a sign around his neck reading ". . . . ." They could fill in the line by heart.

That unpaved parking lot was one of Price's biggest headaches during Musicarnival's first seasons. On rainy nights, Price had to endure more than a soaking while bidding the audience good night; after helping to push the more unfortunate motorists out of the mudholes, he was always the last to leave the lot. Price even consulted novelist and gentleman farmer Louis Bromfield of Mansfield, trying to find a hardier grass to hold up in wet weather. When Musicarnival negotiated a new five-year lease from Thistledown in 1957, a paved parking lot was at the top of its agenda. Splitting the $80,000 outlay with the racetrack, which would use it by day, Bob Bishop ordered asphalt laid down east of the tent for one thousand cars. "We've tried to keep it rustic," observed Price, noting that the blacktopping process would work its way around the apple orchard serving as the preperformance picnic grounds.

While paved parking may have been the most appreciated, it was one of many physical improvements to the Musicarnival plant over the years. Seating capacity was increased several times in response to the emphatic success of what was once viewed as "Price's Folly": from 1,700 the first year, to 1,900 in 1957, and 2,100 by the time of the *Cinderella* premiere. Ultimately 2,561 patrons could be accommodated under the big top. Following the season of the tornado, Price also made sure he had a spare tent stored on the grounds in case it were to be needed before the old one wore out.

Major advancements in production facilities took place prior to the 1964 season. Since there was no backstage in an arena theater, Price sought additional working space in the only direction available: downward. Excavation equipment moved in to provide Musicarnival with a full, nine-foot-deep basement beneath the stage, replacing the old concrete pilings underneath with block walls providing storage space for props and scenery, with three elevators to bring them up to stage level. "It allows for the use of much heavier, more ornate props," explained Peter Bellamy in the *Plain Dealer*. "The new method of scene changing also will eliminate much of the clatter of characters in black clothing running madly up and down the aisles carrying props." It would also allow quick costume changes understage, cutting down even more on traffic in the aisles. At the same time, the depth of the orchestra pit was increased from four feet to seven, improving sightlines for the audience seated behind. Reviewing a show that season, Anderson of the *Press* noted,

"Last night three sidewalk cafe tables, all with chairs and setups, popped up from the basement to the stage level like magic." Never one to let his imagination rest, Price was already dreaming of next installing a revolving stage.

Musicarnival had established itself as a leader in the burgeoning tent theater movement. There were nineteen of them in 1957; a year later Hoyt of the *Plain Dealer* counted twenty-five. "While Broadway keeps shrinking, the summertime tent musicals keep expanding," observed *Saturday Review* magazine that season. Rebecca Franklin in the *New York Times Magazine,* citing the construction of a $500,000 permanent, aluminum-domed arena theater in Fort Worth, Texas, saw the musical arenas doubling in number within another decade.

Price and Bishop's tent was the model most of the new ones hoped to emulate. It led the field by 1958 with a twenty-week season and an annual audience of a quarter-million theatergoers. Bob Bishop thought it was the first tent to have a paved parking lot; John Price was billing Musicarnival as "America's Finest Musical Theatre-in-the-Round." Cleveland's critics didn't dispute it. "For freedom of vision and excellence of acoustics it is probably the finest tent in the United States," stated McDermott in the *Plain Dealer.* National publications tended to confirm it. "Probably one of the best run and most prosperous tents is Cleveland's Musicarnival," wrote David Dachs in *Travel* magazine.

Musicarnival was also paid the unequivocally sincere flattery of imitation. Ridge Bond, leading man of the inaugural production of *Oklahoma!* started his own Melody Circus tent the following summer in Detroit. Price and Bishop were hired as consultants the following year for a new tent in North Tonawanda near Buffalo, New York. Dubbed the Melody Fair, it emulated Musicarnival's perfectly circular design and began sharing leading players and productions with its Cleveland cousin. Price began thinking of a Buffalo-Cleveland-Detroit circuit, with perhaps a second Cleveland tent on the West Side for Clevelanders daunted by the pre–I-480 trip to the far eastern fringe. When Price and Bishop did give Musicarnival a little sister, however, they placed it not on the West Side but in West Palm

Beach, Florida. Opened in 1958, Musicarnival Palm Beach operated during the winter months, which made it possible to share not only productions but also its tent with its Cleveland progenitor.

Bob Bishop, who had once viewed his cousin's Musicarnival prospectus with skepticism, now admitted he had "the theater bug . . . bad." Following a personal tour of the country's tent theaters, Bishop called their managers together in 1955 to form the Musical Arena Theatre Association (MATA). "Sinjun" Terrell was elected its first president, and Bishop vice president. With his solid business experience, however, Bishop became the driving force in the organization and eventually its president. He chaired a committee that concluded the first collective bargaining agreement for stock theater in the history of Actors Equity. "Up until 1958, Equity told us what the salaries would be," explains Price. "Bob forced them legally to recognize MATA and negotiate with us." It was a total reversal of the historical pattern in which management traditionally had to be forced to bargain with labor. According to Price, one of Bishop's most effective weapons was a stutter that eventually could wear down the opposition. Other MATA initiatives included a six-week course for theater managers covering such areas as theatrical accounting, box office mechanics, personnel problems, and "the care and feeding of canvas." "Sometimes," said Bishop, "I get so busy with theater matters that I retain lawyers instead of doing the legal work myself."

With the increasing involvement of Bishop, Musicarnival became more of a family affair than ever. That first-year production of *Show Boat*, with three generations of Prices on stage, was more than a stunt. Not since the days of "Uncle John" Ellsler and the old Academy of Music had Cleveland seen such a theater dynasty as the Price-Bishop clan. Ellsler had managed the academy for twenty years before building the Euclid Avenue Opera House, also assuming character roles in their stock companies. His wife, Euphemia, was the leading lady besides helping with the box office. Their four children were all involved in the family business, either in the front of the house (the two sons) or onstage (the two daughters). The eldest daughter, Euphemia (or Effie), became one of the most successful actresses in nineteenth-century America, famous on Broadway and the road as "Cleveland's Sweetheart."

Like John Ellsler, John Price not only managed his company and theater but took on bit parts as well. "Whenever John could, he would get into the act," observed Bill Boehm, Musicarnival's first director. "He would make a fine contribution, but it had to be in his own style . . . [and] it had to be small, because he had a lot to do." Rusty Charlie in *Guys and Dolls* fell within these criteria, as did the World's Fair barker in *Show Boat*. Others included Baptista in *Kiss Me, Kate,* a drunk in *Wonderful Town,* a street busker in *My Fair Lady,* and the manager of the Washington Senators–Cleveland Indians in *Damn Yankees.* Given his World War II Navy credentials, Price also cast himself as Admiral von Schreiber in *The Sound of Music* and Commander Harbison in *South Pacific* (though in the latter he may have been more temperamentally suited to play the regulation-bending Luther Billis).

Connie Price designed more than three dozen productions for Musicarnival in the early years. Her studio was the Price living room in Bratenahl, where she could keep an eye on the baby, Mat (Philip Mather), and have lunch ready for Jock and Diana when they arrived from school. When she had to be at the tent, Mat went along in a basket. In the 1957 *Die Fledermaus,* Connie made a cameo appearance with all three children in a pantomime scene. Her duties also took her on occasion to New York to pick out costumes for upcoming productions. Family duties gradually kept her more at home, however, especially after the birth of a fourth child, Madeline, in 1960. (Because of a Price family tradition that the births of male children coincided with years in which the Cleveland Indians won the pennant, she was called Mikey—it didn't work that year.) But not even four children could keep Connie out of the theater indefinitely. In 1963 she made her Musicarnival acting debut as an eccentric countess in *Wildcat.*

As for the children, only the two oldest succumbed to the smell of greasepaint. During the first year Jock and Diana appeared on stage as a little boy and girl in *Annie Get Your Gun* and as extras in *Carousel.* Jock recalls later portraying a fan in *Damn Yankees.* Diana eventually appeared in seven shows in all, including a production of *Damn Yankees* at the Palm Beach Musicarnival. Her favorite was *Take Me Along*, in which she had advanced to the name role of Mildred, the protagonist's younger sister. "I was never big on performing," she protests. "It was nothing I ever felt I was good at." Both she and Jock moved instead into Musicarnival's apprentice program, assuming such backstage roles as dresser and sceneshifter. Neither Philip nor Mikey were ever bitten by the theatrical bug, although their grandmother, Emma, and cousin, Bob Bishop, more than made up for their indifference.

But for John Price, as with "Uncle John" Ellsler, the concept of family extended beyond blood to embrace his entire theater company. There was, for one example, his close relationship with Bill Boehm, fellow Western Reserve and Cain Park alumnus. Boehm fondly recalls the collegial atmosphere of the tent's first year. "You didn't call your life your own, and it didn't bother you," he says. "We pretty much had meetings every night." The one exception was Friday night, which was reserved for poker. "Even the ladies would join in," remembers the director. "Then we'd get in the car, put it in automatic, and go home."

Yet four years later, Price felt compelled to let his old college chum go. "It was a little embarrassing," he admits. Having brought in Boehm when neither was sure of the demands of directing in the round, Price now reluctantly concluded that his director wasn't quite up to the task. "I had very few credentials as a director, actually," agrees Boehm. "I was a performer. If someone asked me, I could do it, but I had no training." Fortunately, it didn't mark the end of the friendship, and Boehm would return regularly for acting assignments, including many under his successor.

What made the change almost inevitable for Price was the emergence of a natural talent in his own company. Don Driver (he still spelled his first name with two *n*s then) was on Musicarnival's stage for the opening night *Oklahoma!* in 1954, playing the comic role of Will Parker. Raised on the West Coast, Driver spent World War II in the Navy before breaking into show business as a radio announcer in

Seattle. Having put on a little weight just sitting behind a mike, he decided to take it off by studying under the G. I. Bill at the American School of Ballet in New York. That led to a three-year engagement with the Ballet Russe de Monte Carlo. But Driver wanted to sing and act as well as dance, so he next landed a spot in the chorus of *A Tree Grows in Brooklyn* on Broadway. Prominent roles followed at the New York City Center, where he played Frank in *Show Boat* and Og in *Finian's Rainbow*. John Price happened to catch him in the latter and signed him up for the resident company of Musicarnival.

Driver caught the Cleveland critics' eyes immediately that first season, stealing the show in Musicarnival's production of *Finian's Rainbow*. He also got a chance that summer to reprise his City Center role in *Show Boat,* in which he was commended for restoring the vaudevillian "I Might Fall Back on You" to the Jerome Kern score. By 1961, the fair-haired, boyish-looking actor had appeared in twenty-seven roles under the tent, specializing in such comic turns as Nathan Detroit in *Guys and Dolls,* Luther Billis in *South Pacific,* and Applegate in *Damn Yankees.* What he seemed to like best were comparatively minor parts to which he could add an over-the-top twist, such as the Indian in *Naughty Marietta* and the foppish Lutz in *The Student Prince.* "Lutz has a basic belief that everybody else is a fool, a bore and dreadfully unmannered," Driver explained to a reporter. "He says things to people that members of the audience would like to say to people but don't. He is commenting, for the audience, on the affectations of the society around him."

If he hoped to keep him, Price clearly had to give a talent like Driver's more scope. Even after becoming the resident director, Driver continued to act and began doctoring scripts to make them more stageable. For *Naughty Marietta* in 1960, in the words of Driver's program bio, "He not only directed the whole show as usual, but rewrote the fifty-year-old script into a delightful entertainment enhancing the show's original script and charm, contributed the lyrics for one of the new character songs, and brought down the house every night with his performance as the Indian." Driver seemed to thrive under the workload, praising the "truly creative atmosphere" at Musicarnival and crediting Price for granting him the artistic leeway to implement his ideas. "He was just about the greatest director I've ever seen," says Price in turn of his protégé. He talked up the director at every opportunity, one result being the *Cinderella* assignment from the Rodgers and Hammerstein organization.

Though he'd be the last to express any regrets, Price may have promoted Driver right out of Musicarnival. In the off seasons the director had created a lucrative business producing industrial shows in New York. After *Cinderella* he understandably harbored ambitions to make his creative mark in the New York theater. "Don got very hot," recalls Price. "I just couldn't afford him anymore." After nine seasons, five of them as director, Don Driver left the tent.

For his third—and last—director of the production years, Price once again reached into his own company. Otto Pirchner was a nephew of Herman Pirchner, Price's old boss at the Alpine Village. While still attending Euclid High School, he was invited by Bill Boehm, another family friend, to join Musicarnival's apprentice program in 1955. Over the following few summers young Pirchner learned musical theater from the bottom up, starting in the box office and switchboard and eventually moving up the rungs of properties manager, assistant stage manager, set designer, singer, and dancer. By the time of his promotion to director, Pirchner had worked on more than sixty Musicarnival productions.

During the off-seasons, Pirchner studied for two years at the Cleveland Institute of Art and studied dance on a scholarship at the Ballet Theater in New York. In 1962 he toured for nine months in the national company of *Carnival,* which later happened to be his inaugural directing assignment at Musicarnival. Still only twenty-five, he was said to be the youngest director of a major professional theater in the nation. In that first 1963 season as director, Pirchner also did double duty as his own set designer. Like his predecessor Don Driver, Pirchner's ultimate goal was to direct on Broadway.

There were changes in positions other than the stage director too. After giving the beat for Musicarnival's first six seasons, maestro Boris

Kogan was succeeded by a revolving door full of conductors. Wilson Stone, a former studio composer for Paramount Pictures, led the orchestra for the 1960 season. Continuity was restored with Lawrence Brown, who conducted over the following three summers. A veteran of the St. Louis Municipal Opera, Brown began his tenure by not only conducting but also by writing special ballet music for *Cinderella*. Musicarnival provided him with a podium and a wife as well. Brown met Susan Johnson during the run of *Gypsy* and subsequently married the actress. Two native Akronites presided over the pit for Musicarnival's final two production seasons. Dickson Hughes, former choral director for the Kenley Players in Warren, conducted in 1964, followed by Wally Harper, a former Julliard student, in 1965.

There was an even greater turnover of scenic designers after Connie Price retired to raise her family. In 1959, however, John Price secured the services of Paul Rodgers, a veteran of the Pasadena Playhouse and, more recently, the Cleveland Play House. Rodgers did the sets for such Musicarnival productions as *Kismet, The Great Waltz, Cinderella,* and *Take Me Along*. Assisting Rodgers in 1961 was another member of the Cleveland Play House staff, Eugene Hare, who took over as designer of that season's closing musical, *South Pacific,* and stayed on to design later shows such as *Fiorello!* In 1961 Price had hired a twenty-year-old prodigy from Erie, Pennsylvania, as set designer for Palm Beach Musicarnival. Two years later Edward Graczyk II was designing *The Music Man* for the Cleveland operation, and he became Musicarnival's principal scenic designer for the last two production years.

Price was fortunate to find two reliable assistants for the unsung but vital position of stage manager. Lawrence Vincent joined Musicarnival in its second season, playing de Becque's servant Henry in the initial production of *South Pacific*. Holding a master's degree in theater from Western Reserve University (later Case Western Reserve University), he headed the drama department at Edinboro State College in Pennsylvania during the winters. As stage manager at Musicarnival during the early years, Vincent continued to play small parts such as the Chamberlain in *Cinderella* and Grobert in *Carnival*. He also directed the 1959 revival of *Kismet* and later was appointed director of the Musicarnival School.

Toward the end of the production years, Price took on a pixyish twenty-year-old from Illinois named Judith Daykin. Since she couldn't afford the full four-year theater course, she had crowded all the theater classes she could into two years at the University of Iowa. Price hired her as assistant set designer at the Palm Beach Musicarnival, where she also played the elderly Lady Beekman in *Gentlemen Prefer Blondes*. Brought up to the Cleveland tent, she filled the positions of publicity assistant, stage manager, production coordinator, and assistant to the producer. A directing assignment with the Hudson Players for *Anything Goes* broadened her experience. As if she needed to prove anything else, Daykin also became the ace of the Musicarnival softball team's pitching staff.

Since Price maintained a resident stock company through the production years, actors were naturally part of Musicarnival's extended family. Invariably Price would fill the chorus and minor players from local talent and hold auditions in New York for his leads. Most of the leads were not quite household names but veterans of road company shows, known mainly, perhaps, to musical comedy connoisseurs. Generally they stayed for more than one show a summer and then returned for several summers. Comedienne Joan Kibrig, for example, was on hand for not only the first but the following ten seasons, playing in *Guys and Dolls* (twice); *Wonderful Town; Kiss Me, Kate; Can-Can;* and *Bells Are Ringing*. Another regular was Susan Johnson, who progressed from young Annie Oakley in 1954's *Annie Get Your Gun* to Mama Rose in 1962's *Gypsy*.

Though committed to avoiding the star system, Price would go after a name if suitable for the part—and within his budget. Juanita Hall and Beverly Sills were early examples. "I had a lid," reveals Price. "The only time I broke it was for Beverly Sills, and I made her promise not to tell." (Now it can be told: for the soprano's 1955 *Die Fledermaus*, it was $350 a week.) For *The Great Waltz* the producer imported another operatic voice, Irra Petina. In 1958 Martyn Green, former star of England's famed D'Oyly Carte Opera Company, was in residence at the Warrensville Heights tent. Though he didn't have a chance to give any of his legendary Gilbert and Sullivan interpretations, he gave memorable performances as Og in *Finian's Rainbow* and Captain Hook in *Peter Pan.*

Tenor Robert Rounesville was another rare example of the star system during the production years. Price first brought him in for revivals of *The Student Prince* in 1958 and 1959. Rounesville was well known for his appearances in film versions of *Carousel* and *The Tales of Hoffmann* and in the title role of the Leonard Bernstein cult classic, *Candide.* "This gentleman not only has a fluid control of his highly pleasant voice but his diction is extraordinarily good," said Stan Anderson in the *Press* of Rounesville's Prince Karl Franz at Musicarnival. "Rounesville treats everybody in the tent like a special customer." When the tenor returned a few years later for *The Merry Widow,* however, he displayed a bit of star temperament. Diana Price tells of a nightly skirmish between Rounesville and his co-star Claire Alexander as to who would take the final curtain call. "Ladies first," said Rounesville, to which Alexander replied, "No, Bob, I am the star. This is *The Merry WIDOW.*" "Claire," rebutted the tenor, "they PAY to see me."

In 1960 Price cast two seasoned veterans of the New York City Opera in the Harold Rome musical, *Fanny.* Bass Joshua Hecht assumed the role of Cesar, originally written for Ezio Pinza, while Al Medinets took the part of Cesar's old friend Panisse, a role originated by Walter Slezak. "In the continental manner," said Mooney of Hecht and Medinets in the *Press,* "they feud, fight and fuss all during the proceedings, only to tear your heart out in a deathbed farewell." Hecht made a memorable Dr. Engel later that season to Robert Rounesville's *Student Prince* and returned in Musicarnival's last production season to undertake another Pinza role as Emile de Becque in *South Pacific.* Medinets, under the abbreviated stage handle of Al Dennis, became probably the most familiar face on Musicarnival's stage during the next few years. He stopped the show in *Take Me Along* for his comic duet with Renee Orin, "I Get Embarrassed." He

LUCILLE BENSON

AL MEDINETS

JOSHUA HECHT

CELESTE CRONISE

HARRY THEYARD

LAURIE FRANK

Fanny, the Harold Rome musical caricatured here by the *Press*'s Jim Herron, displayed the depth of Musicarnival's reparatory company during the production years. Hecht and Medinets (later Dennis) "feud, fight, and fuss all during the proceedings," wrote one critic, "only to tear your heart out in a deathbed farewell." *Cleveland Press,* August 2, 1960.

was the king in *Cinderella,* a Mormon in *Paint Your Wagon,* and the sheriff in *The Red Mill.* Having played Stewpot in an earlier revival, he got to play Billis in the last *South Pacific* of the production years, teamed once again with Joshua Hecht. *Plain Dealer* critic Robert Finn overheard one departing theatergoer say apropos of Dennis, "Is there anything the man can't do?" Added Finn, "Second the motion."

Backing up such principal players was a never-ending stream of local talent and theatrical hopefuls. Some such as Wayne Mack were veterans of Cain Park and the Cleveland 500. Nolan Bell came from Karamu to appear in *Kiss Me, Kate,* while Richard Oberlin of the Cleveland Play House could be seen in *The King and I.* Native Clevelander Frank Shaw Stevens returned from New York in the 1950s to act at both the Play House and Musicarnival, taking on such roles at the latter as the Starkeeper in *Carousel.* Old-timer Walter Davis, who once managed his own Finger Lakes Lyric Circus in upstate New York, was hired by Price for *Flower Drum Song* in 1962.

Imogene Bliss was seen in a variety of small parts during the early seasons. Native Clevelander Providence Hollander broke out of the chorus in *The Red Mill* to portray Elizabeth Woodling in *Paint Your Wagon*. From neighboring Maple Heights, a young dancer named Ernie Horvath managed to land the part of a servant in *Cinderella*. Another dancer from the same suburb, Frank Baloga (stage name, Brooks), still recalls John Price's "You're in!" after auditioning in 1964. Akronite Marian Mercer, fresh out of the University of Michigan, joined the Musicarnival chorus in 1958 and soon was singing Ellie in *Show Boat*. In New York three years later she inherited the lead in the off-Broadway hit *Little Mary Sunshine*. A little later Robert Miragliotta came up from the Akron suburb of Wadsworth via Baldwin-Wallace College to join the chorus and fill bit parts at Musicarnival.

In order to keep the talent flowing, Price instituted a Musicarnival School in 1956, consisting of a fellowship and an apprenticeship program. For the former, he and Larry Vincent went to see Price's old drama instructor at Western Reserve University, Barclay Leathem. They came up with a program in which drama students would receive up to six hours' credit from the university for practical experience at Musicarnival, ranging from scavenging the city for props to taking tickets at the door. In return for these services, Musicarnival picked up their tuition tabs and paid them weekly stipends. Lending the process academic respectability was a series of thrice-weekly seminars conducted by Musicarnival staff or visiting authorities. In 1957, for example, seminars were held by Price, Bob Bishop, Boris Kogan, Don Driver, and Irra Petina among others. Theodore Bikel, Sammy Davis Jr., and Bill Cosby took their turns behind the lectern in later summers. John Price's "cultural kindergarten" had taken on a graduate school.

Alongside the fellowship program, Musicarnival also accepted up to a dozen apprentices annually on much the same terms minus the college credit. They were given fair warning that they would get "all the 'dirty jobs' in the theatre" and would be expected "to perform them to perfection." (Price was wont to boast that he had been Cain Park's first janitor—"and the best.") Recalling an apprentice named Michael Tebelak, Frank Baloga says, "I remember him as spilling a lot of turpentine." Today, Tebelak is remembered as the author of

Seminars were a standard feature of the Musicarnival School organized by John Price and stage manager Larry Vincent. Fellowship students and apprentices were given instruction in practical theater conditions by staff members and visiting artists such as Price, Boris Kogan, and Irra Petina. John L. Price Jr. Musicarnival Archives, Cleveland Public Library.

Godspell. Apprentices along with fellowship students also gained practical stage experience by putting on their own shows. Diana Price, who served as a "techie" with brother Jock, was directed by Judy Daykin in a production of *The Drunkard.* Later apprentices were responsible for a Children's Theatre at Musicarnival, putting on weekly afternoon shows such as *Hansel and Gretel; You're a Good Man, Charlie Brown;* and *Adventures in Wonderland.*

Not surprisingly Musicarnival took on an ambience more redolent of a campus than the neon and tinsel of 42nd Street. It was reinforced by the bucolic setting with its adjacent picnic grounds, used not only by patrons before the shows but by the Musicarnival company for relaxing during rehearsal breaks and socializing. The Women's Committee continued serving their opening night buffets for the players and also provided Musicarnival with everything from volunteer seamstresses to ushers. "[T]here isn't another theatre of this type around the country completely and openly commercial in its inception that has anything like the community participation and acceptance that Musicarnival has," Price told one of his seminars. "We've never paid a penny to an usher since we've been open." Many local families even opened their homes to visiting show people, providing room and board not only for extra income but also for the up-close exposure to some of the glamour of show business.

Camaraderie was also promoted by special events, such as the baseball game between the Musicarnival company and that of the Great Lakes Shakespeare Festival. The pretext, if one were needed, was the four hundredth anniversary in 1964 of Shakespeare's birth, in honor of which Shakespeare buff Price scheduled the Bard-derived musicals *Kiss Me, Kate* and *The Boys from Syracuse. Plain Dealer* critic Peter Bellamy umpired the contest, which was played out on a nearby diamond at Warrensville Heights High School. Thanks to the clutch relief pitching of Judy Daykin ("She had control and several curves," wrote Bellamy), the Musicarnival nine prevailed, 28–14.

For thespians in search of less rigorous sport, there was always Thistledown next door. Price recalls that his first maestro, Boris Kogan, was a dedicated player on the ponies, conducting rehearsals with one eye on the score and the other on the track results. In a revival of *Guys and Dolls,* former boxer "Slapsie Maxie" Rosenbloom was cast in the showcase role of Big Jule. Price remembers bumping into him trudging back to the tent from the track, with his cauliflower ears and "his nose . . . all over his face." "How'd you do, Maxie?" asked the producer. "Ah did pretty well," replied Rosenbloom in his best pugilese. "Gaht mah cah-fahr home."

Across the street from the tent was a new Warrensville Heights City Hall. Once suspicious of the "wicked stage," city fathers now regarded Musicarnival as definitely a good neighbor. A 3 percent admissions tax undoubtedly helped bring them around, but Price also helped sponsor such community activities as youth concerts and Police Athletic League benefits. Official acceptance took the form of a formal "Resolution of Appreciation" issued by the City Council in 1972, which observed that "through the efforts of John Price, the

Located in a corner of Thistledown racetrack, Musicarnival had no problem borrowing a horse for a cameo appearance in *Guys and Dolls*. Frank Leo appeared as one of the guys, but his equine companion received no billing. John L. Price Jr. Musicarnival Archives, Cleveland Public Library.

City of Warrensville Heights has been placed on the entertainment map throughout the United States."

Even more important to Price than official sanction, however, was the continued approval of his audience. He kept up-to-date files on individual subscribers and generally answered complaints personally. When one regular opening-night patron failed to show for the first night of *The Music Man*, Price sent flowers and a note to

Dorothy Frankel of Shaker Heights. "The season doesn't seem properly opened without you," he wrote. Happily, Mrs. Frankel wasn't ill, just out of town. She was definitely worth the producer's attention, having attended Musicarnival twenty-six times in the opening season alone and often bringing half a dozen friends to the theater with her. That she was the aunt of *Cleveland Press* television critic Jim Frankel didn't hurt either.

Group bookings were also important for the Musicarnival box office. Tickets were sold in blocks ranging from twenty-five to one thousand seats. For the opening of *Cinderella,* the Holstein-Friesian Association Convention took 750 seats (though *Oklahoma!* might have been a more suitable show for that crowd). Other groups buying blocks that season included the Cleveland YMCA, the downtown Kiwanis, the Lutheran Children's Aid Society, the Arena Players of Garfield Heights, and the Western Reserve Women's Republican Club. Depending on the size of the party, prices for group sales sliced from 5 to 20 percent off the box office scale, a savings that might have either been passed on to the members of the group or used for fundraising purposes. The Cuyahoga Falls Rotary Club, for example, turned its theater party into a benefit for crippled children.

Efforts to expand Musicarnival's audience occasionally went beyond the presentation of musical shows. There was an art exhibit in 1957, featuring works by such "Cleveland School" artists as Ed and Thelma Winter, Edris Eckhardt, Victor Schreckengost, William Grauer, and Paul Travis. During the 1960s Sunday afternoon jazz concerts became an annual fixture in the tent. Though not personally an aficionado, Price recognized the contribution of such figures as Louis Armstrong, Dave Brubeck, Stan Kenton, and Lionel Hampton to American music. He booked them all as part of Musicarnival's All-Star Jazz Concerts, along with such other combos as the Dukes of Dixieland, George Shearing, and Erroll Garner. Though unnecessary in Cleveland, a cancellation clause in Duke Ellington's contract in the event of any audience segregation "because of race or color" is a reminder of the temper of the times. Somewhat unsure of the jazz audience, however, Price hired security for the initial concert but

Musicarnival's Sunday afternoon All-Star Jazz Concerts brought immortals such as Louis Armstrong to jam under the big top. John L. Price Jr. Musicarnival Archives, Cleveland Public Library.

discovered he might have saved the expense. The "jazz crowd," he told a writer for *Fine Arts* magazine, was "more polite, more literate, more alert and attentive than the audiences who come for the regular musical fare."

Through annual audience surveys, Price kept informed of his clientele's tastes and concerns. Parking was still a cause for complaint, though more for the fifty-cent charge than for the quality of the service. "No other place have we had to pay to park at a theater," was one comment. Not surprisingly, there were also complaints about "inadequate toilet facilities," especially for the ladies. Box office and ushers received high marks, but the refreshment stand was criticized for high prices and long lines. "Your coffee could be better," added a few. The majority of the audience found the new sound system an improvement, though some still found hearing difficult "when actors facing opposite direction." There were also a few complaints about the gravel flooring underneath the seats. "I'm tired of shining shoes," said one.

Concerning the shows themselves, one respondent chided, "Some costumes too scanty." Another, pointedly identifying himself as "MALE PATRON," found fault with "Too much use of hell, damn, etc. [and] so much reference to sex. I'm not a prude," he insisted. "I have 6 children and enjoy good clean fun." Sounding out his audience again about opera, Price got numerous replies that they didn't understand it. "I prefer music with a beat," said one. Others replied that they just didn't feel that a tent was the proper place for opera, but a few expressed disappointment over the cancellation of plans for *The Tales of Hoffmann*. "What happened? Pressure from the 'big wheels'?" asked one. There were a few gripes about the long drive from the West Side, though one fan from much farther west wrote, "Enjoy shows, will attend more next year, even though from Toledo." Even that was topped by another, who commented "Wonderful entertainment, drive hundreds of miles for a performance." Of all the accolades, however, the one best calculated to warm the producer's heart was the one that read "John Price has done more for Cleveland theatre than any other group or individual before him."

One regular survey question asked patrons to check off or write in shows they would like to see in Musicarnival's future seasons. A glance at the following summer's schedule would indicate that John Price was listening. In the 1959 survey, for example, the top audience choices were as follows:

1. *The Music Man*
2. *Pal Joey*

3. *West Side Story*
4. *The Vagabond King*
5. *Fanny*
6. *Naughty Marietta*
7. *The Chocolate Soldier*
8. *Anything Goes*

All of the above, except *The Music Man* and *The Chocolate Soldier,* showed up in the repertoire for the 1960 season. *The Music Man* followed in 1962 as soon as Musicarnival could get the rights. One of Price's perennial disappointments was the failure of any Gilbert and Sullivan operetta to break into the top of the list. "I love Gilbert and Sullivan," he says. "I would have loved to do it, but the audience wasn't there." Martyn Green had been there in 1958, and Cleveland thus lost an opportunity to hear him sing one of the patter songs that made him immortal.

Revivals remained frequent during the last of the production years at Musicarnival. *South Pacific* had been given its fourth showing by 1965; *The Student Prince* and *Show Boat* had three apiece. Shows given double exposure in the tent included *Kiss Me, Kate; Gentlemen Prefer Blondes; Can-Can;* and *The Desert Song.* But with Vietnam heating up, not even *South Pacific* was sacred anymore. "We're particularly cynical about romantic interludes in the midst of war and horror," demurred Dick Shippy in the *Akron Beacon Journal.* And in order to bring Romberg's *The Desert Song* in tune with the sixties, director Don Driver decided to rework it as a self-conscious travesty of operetta conventions. "Everybody strikes deliberately stilted poses to illustrate how amusingly quaint old operetta singers seemed in acting—were they really so bad?—during that era," observed Glenn Pullen in the *Plain Dealer.*

There were also some newcomers during those years—1962 was a very good one for premieres, with *Flower Drum Song, Bye Bye Birdie, Gypsy, Fiorello!* and *Do Re Mi* all making their Musicarnival bows. *Carnival, Wildcat,* and *The Unsinkable Molly Brown* came in the following summer. *The Music Man* made its long-awaited debut in 1962 with Monte Amundsen as Marian the librarian and set changes by cast members integrated into the action by director Driver. Two years later Price was finally able to offer the two biggest musicals of their era, *The Sound of Music* and *My Fair Lady*. Summing up the latter in the *Cleveland Press,* Tony Mastroianni observed, "In short, everyone rose to the level of the material, which is a high level indeed." As for *The Sound of Music,* it did well enough to merit a revival in the very next season.

One of the freshest new shows of the period was *110 in the Shade,* a musical version of N. Richard Nash's *The Rainmaker* by Tom Jones and Harvey Schmidt, creators of *The Fantasticks.* The story of a con man who claims he can bring an end to a searing western drought, *110 in the Shade* opened, as luck would have it, on a June night when the Musicarnival tent was hit by a terrific thunderstorm. After a long rain delay, the action happened to resume at the point where the skeptical heroine confronts the self-styled rainmaker with the line, "Well, I bet you feel real pleased with yourself." It brought the second-biggest laugh of the evening, topped only by the rainmaker's rejoinder, "Any reason I shouldn't be?" Later in that 1965 season Price tried to capitalize on the current folk-music fad by resurrecting a twenty-year-old show called *Sing Out Sweet Land.* Al Dennis and B. J. Ward anchored this anthology of such traditional tunes as "Blue Tail Fly" and "Camptown Races." It may have been charming in its day, but that day was past.

Musicarnival had opened in the middle of the golden age of the American musical theater. Twelve years later, the golden age was over. Oscar Hammerstein II had died in 1960. Cole Porter and Frank Loesser would also be gone by the end of the decade. Frederick Loewe and Irving Berlin opened their last shows in 1960 and 1962, respectively. Perhaps the greatest loss occurred about the same time, when the great young hope of the musical theater, Leonard Bernstein, abandoned Broadway for Carnegie Hall as conductor of the New York Philharmonic. A few young talents such as Sheldon Harnick, Jerry Bock, and Stephen Sondheim were beginning to emerge, but the giants of the genre were gone.

WITH TWO SHOWS, "TOSCA" AND "SOUTH PACIFIC" BOTH NOW IN REHEARSAL AT MUSICARNIVAL, DULL MOMENTS ARE SCARCE...

FOR INSTANCE, AT ONE TIME YOU CAN HEAR AN ARIA FROM "TOSCA," THE PUT-PUT OF A GAS MOWER, SONGS BY RODGERS AND HAMMERSTEIN...

MICHAEL POLLACK DIRECTS IN SHORTS WHILE "TOSCA" STARS BEVERLY SILLS AND WILLIAM CHAPMAN GO IN FOR RELAXED REHEARSAL...

STAGE MANAGER MARTHA HANDLEY SAVES HER NERVES FOR OPENING NIGHT MONDAY...

STRAY BIRDS TEST THE STARS' TEMPERS...

EVERYONE RIDES BIKES —EVEN WHILE STUDYING LINES...

"TOSCA" MUSICAL CHIEF BORIS KOGAN HAS HIS OWN COOLING SYSTEM...

"TAKE 15" MEANS DIFFERENT THINGS TO DIFFERENT PEOPLE.

"Summertime and the livin' is easy," as Ira Gershwin put it in *Porgy and Bess,* might also have described Musicarnival during the early production years. Artist Jim Herron captured the semirural ambiance that prevailed before the area became overdeveloped. *Cleveland Press,* June 22, 1957.

John Price had long been aware of the need for new material. "How many times can you do *Oklahoma! South Pacific,* and *Guys and Dolls?*" he asks. To fill out his seasons he had experimented with grand opera and tried to revive the operettas that had been Cain Park's mainstay. He encouraged Don Driver to adapt *Cinderella* for the round and called on others to create shows for the tents. Lately Bob Bishop had joined the campaign, demanding that Broadway relinquish its "monopoly" of new hit shows. At the end of 1963, however, the forty-seven-year-old Musicarnival president was discovered by his gardener in his Hunting Valley bedroom, dead of a self-inflicted gunshot wound. He left a note telling of depression and ill health. "Bob always was a somber person," says his cousin-in-law Price. Not even his latent passion for the theater could bring him out completely.

Not long afterward, Price could count only three charter members among his staff of seventy-five—concertmaster Ben Silverberg, electrician Ben Kleinman, and producer John Price. By the end of the twelfth season he had presented ninety productions of sixty-seven different shows. Only two of them—*Porgy and Bess* and *West Side Story*—had been "package" shows brought in from outside. For the production years, however, as with Cinderella, the clock was approaching midnight.

4

The Package Years:
From Benny to Burlesque

We believe in balanced productions. We will not succumb to the
star system. You can't get stars to come in to rehearse for a week.
When you have a star who comes in the day before the show
starts, you have a freak show.

John Price was holding forth in the offices of the *Cleveland Plain
Dealer* on the eve of Musicarnival's 1962 season. "When his
trained voice expands to full volume on his favorite topic, everybody can't help but listen," reported drama critic Peter Bellamy. "The
Women's department, the Sunday magazine staff, and the Sunday copy
desk all got the message clearly. . . . Indeed, his full-throated perora-
tion on what he considers the hellish evils of the star system in summer musical theaters had Emerson Batdorff, *Plain Dealer* columnist,
all but reverberating on the other side of a row of steel lockers."

It was no straw man Price was swinging at, either. Musicarnival's
main competition happened to be a theater fifty miles east of Cleveland in Warren, Ohio, where an impresario named John Kenley had
been filling an indoor hall even larger than Price's tent. Every bit as
much a showman as Price, Kenley's success formula was the very

star system Price was denouncing. Since 1958 he had offered such billings as Dan Dailey in *Guys and Dolls,* Barbara Eden in *Lady in the Dark,* and Howard Keel in *Kismet.* These weren't the musical theater veterans Price had been casting for his leads; they were for the most part movie stars and television personalities with national followings. "It is the wives who generally determine what shows they and their husbands are going to see," expounded Kenley in illustration of his casting philosophy.

That philosophy may have worked splendidly for John Kenley, but it wasn't John Price's idea of theater. "There are not enough really qualified musical stars for all the summer theaters that want them," he told Bellamy and everyone else within earshot. "Once you condition an audience to see a star instead of a truly fine and balanced production, it won't come except for the star." Price had the backing of Musicarnival president Bob Bishop, who had maintained, "In my mind stars are only actors with publicity and greedy agents. The show's the thing with us."

But Bob Bishop was gone not long afterwards. By 1965 Musicarnival Palm Beach was gone too. It had never achieved the success of its Cleveland counterpart, which had supported its Florida offshoot for much of its eight years of operation. According to Price, the main liability of the southern Musicarnival was a disadvantageous location. "If we had built in Fort Lauderdale, we would have been in clover," he maintains. (Unfortunately, there had been no southern version of Howard Whipple Green to tell him that.) By closing down in Palm Beach he cut his losses, but the Cleveland operation nonetheless inherited the Florida tent's debts.

Other considerations were working to wear down Price's resistance to the star system. For one thing, the supply of new musicals was growing ever more constrictive. Although two huge new hits, *Hello, Dolly!* and *Fiddler on the Roof,* opened on Broadway in 1964, rather than offer a solution they paradoxically became part of the problem. Production costs had skyrocketed to the point that only shows with the most positive receptions could establish themselves for a profitable run. The result was a blockbuster syndrome in which a handful of certified smashes such as *My Fair Lady, Hello, Dolly!* and *Fiddler* were guaranteed record-breaking runs of many years— tying up the best theaters, monopolizing the tourist trade, and consequently making it all the harder for newer works to break into the charmed circle.

Not only was the theater changing, but the audience was undergoing its own transformation. By 1960 the vast majority of American homes had television, and the upstart medium was already being given credit for deciding a national election. More relevant to Musicarnival's fortunes were the variety-style entertainment shows that dominated viewing habits during the era, such as Milton Berle's *Texaco Star Theater,* Ed Sullivan's *Toast of the Town,* and Sid Caesar and Imogene Coca's *Your Show of Shows.* It was the type of entertainment, along with the guilty pleasure of gambling, that also began luring Americans to a desert way station in Nevada. Clevelanders could avail themselves of another new industry, passenger airlines, to view some of their favorite television personalities live, between sessions at the blackjack tables in Las Vegas.

In his 1960 audience survey, Price asked his patrons for their opinion of Musicarnival's policy of "emphasizing quality in *all* phases of production and casting leads on merit, rather than on the basis of glamourous star name value." Granted, the wording may have been slightly loaded, but 90 percent of the respondents expressed approval of the no-stars policy. "I like Hugh Downs, but only as an announcer," commented one, "not as an M. C. or an actor." Those who took the trouble to add comments, however, often qualified their approval with a caveat. "Yes, but a big name now and then would be fun," wrote one. "Yes and No," commented another, "I believe that occasionally a name star should be brought in to attract people who have never come here." "Two or three times feature a name star. It is good show business to do so," said a third.

Those who disagreed with the policy made pointed comparisons with Musicarnival's competition. "No, for the price you should have top performers as at Warren," commented one. "Some stars have talent and might draw well for you as at Warren," added another. One response which might have especially arrested Price's attention stated "I think Cleveland is ready for a change—name stars." It was signed by Frank Griesinger, one of his own directors.

As a family enterprise and a resident stock company, John Price's Musicarnival bore favorable comparison with the grand old man of Cleveland theater, John Ellsler of the Academy of Music. Now Price faced comparison with Ellsler in a less fortunate respect. Shortly after moving into his new Euclid Avenue Opera House in 1875, Ellsler began to confront the threat of what became known as the "combination company." Guest stars, who had formerly come to appear in lead roles with Ellsler's stock company in support, now began arriving with complete productions featuring lavish sets, spectacular effects, and their own supporting casts. Unable to compete against the glamour of these attractions, Ellsler disbanded his company and eventually lost his theater.

Nearly a century later, John Price faced a similar challenge. "The outlook for the 1965 season is not so bright as was that of 1964, when we had four brand new shows to offer," the producer reported to his board early in 1965. With *110 in the Shade* and *A Funny Thing Happened on the Way to the Forum* as his only fresh offerings, he proposed to fall back on more revivals (*The Sound of Music, Show Boat,* etc.) and aggressive marketing to save the season. Besides increasing subscription sales "plus broader promotion of jazz concerts and other special one-shot attractions," Price also hoped to stimulate group sales in such Greater Cleveland corporations as Ohio Bell, Timken, and Republic Steel. "This, in short," he summed up, "is the season when we pass, punt, and pray!"

Reporting to his board a year later, however, Price summarized the 1965 season as "the most disastrous of the 12 we have experienced here in Cleveland." One weekly gross of $9,818.40 had been the lowest since the opening year of Musicarnival. "And it was on a good production!" he insisted, comparing Musicarnival's *110 in the Shade* favorably with the Broadway original. "Well," he observed wryly in reference to the previous year's report, "our passes were intercepted, our punts were blocked, and we were preyed upon!" Nevertheless, despite a loss of $57,500 on the season, the producer still wasn't ready to look to the stars, placing his hopes for 1966 on the availability of such recent shows as *Oliver!* and *How to Succeed in Business without Really Trying.*

A month later, however, the board received a reality check from Musicarnival's accounting firm, Lutz and Carr. Edward O. Lutz reported that the "matured" tents all faced similar problems of rising costs, fewer musicals, and "public apathy resulting principally from the fact that the novelty of the tent theater has worn thin." Adoption of the "star system" was essential, in his opinion, and the board concurred. Noting for the record "that artistry is necessarily being sacrificed to practicalities," Price made the vote unanimous. "Then it was either we went to the star system and bring in star packages or we fold the tent," is how he explains the decision.

According to the revised game plan for 1966, then, Musicarnival would not be casting its own shows that season but instead booking attractions packaged for a circuit including four other tents in Buffalo, New York; Wallingford, Connecticut; Warwick, Rhode Island; and Framingham, Massachusetts. In an equally sweeping departure, fewer than half the shows would be book musicals; the rest would be variety entertainments headlined by such marquee names as Mike Douglas, Jerry Lewis, and Jack Benny. Even book musicals such as *Carousel* and *Oliver!* would be star-driven.

Before Musicarnival could open the first of its package shows, however, it had to reach an agreement with the Stagehands Union. During the production years, the tent had managed to get along with only one union stagehand, an electrician. What little scenery there was could be easily handled by non-union apprentices. With Musicarnival moving to the star system, however, Stagehands Local 27 contended that what had formerly been a semiprofessional operation was now fully professional and needed two additional union technicians. They reinforced their demand by placing pickets around

A signboard on Warrensville Center Road served as Musicarnival's marquee. This one proclaimed the coming world premiere of *A Joyful Noise* during the first of the package years. John L. Price Jr. Musicarnival Archives, Cleveland Public Library.

the theater and prevailing on Local 765 of the Treasurers and Ticket Sellers Union to refuse to handle Musicarnival tickets at the downtown Burrows outlet. Price, always ambivalent in his feelings about unions, countered with a $100,000 damage suit in U.S. District Court, charging the unions with illegal picketing and a secondary boycott. On the day before opening, a settlement was reached by which Musicarnival agreed to take on a union sound man for the coming season and possibly an additional member the next.

That cleared the stage for folk singer Harry Belafonte to kick off the new era on June 6, 1966. "While it is certainly sad that no resident producing company is now operating at Musicarnival," observed Robert Finn in the *Cleveland Plain Dealer*, "it is hard to argue with the success of last night's occasion." Unlike many headliners, Belafonte was on stage practically the entire evening, delivering a balanced medley of his signature calypso songs, folk ballads, spirituals, and the social protest numbers then coming into vogue. While Tony Mastroianni thought he might be able to name a dozen singers with better voices, the *Cleveland Press* critic thought that Belafonte had to be judged on factors other than raw talent. "This is not casual artistry," he wrote. "This is polished, perfected, calculated and highly commercial. . . . It is the charm of a slick and highly palatable adaption of his material for popular consumption."

It had been a near miss with the last-minute union settlement, but John Price's biggest regret must have been that he had only been able to book Belafonte for a single week. Tickets were scarce for the remainder of the engagement, which opened a sixteen-week tour for the singer. Most of the shows that followed, whether book musicals or variety programs, were also scheduled for one-week runs. Television personality Mike Douglas followed Belafonte into the tent with a show that included comedian Frank Fontaine and a musical group called the Bitter End Singers. It was like old-home week for Douglas, whose daytime television program had its beginnings at Cleveland's Channel 3 before being moved to Philadelphia. "Mike knows the people and the people know him," reported *Press* television critic Bill Barrett. "At his opening in the tent Monday night, they stood up to clap when he took his final bow." On the *Press* drama page, Stan Anderson was somewhat less adulatory. "TV personalities took over much of the summer theater scene a few years ago and the trend now is to put them into a night club routine," read his capsule review. "This is a show for TV addicts and assorted squares. Highly successful in this genre," he added for what it was worth.

Other variety acts that summer included comedian Jerry Lewis, who appeared with a singing group named the Skylarks, a dance act known as the Nicholas Brothers, and the Wiere Brothers comedy team. Needing no supporting acts were the King Family Singers, a television clan of brothers, sisters, and in-laws who could fill the Musicarnival stage with thirty-seven performers, all related. A more intimate family act was billed as "An Evening with Robert Goulet and Carol Lawrence," in which the husband-and-wife singing team was backed by comedian Norm Crosby.

"Well!" Though his violin got no respect at Musicarnival, ageless comedian Jack Benny could hold an audience with no more than a wordless expression of exasperation. John L. Price Jr. Musicarnival Archives, Cleveland Public Library.

One of the highlights of the season was a midsummer appearance by ageless comedian Jack Benny, who brought along a young singer named Wayne Newton. The original "thirty-something," Benny (then seventy-two and not counting) came prepared with a line just in case rain were to come leaking through the Musicarnival tent. "Anybody but me would give you your money back," was what he planned to say, but apparently the opportunity never presented itself. His supporting cast also included a violin prodigy named Doris Dodge, who easily managed to outduel him at his favorite instrument. "Play 'Getting to Know You' the way it was written," Benny finally snapped at the ten-year-old in mock exasperation. "He's funny more for the delivery than the content," commented Dick Shippy in the *Akron Beacon Journal.* "A master showman."

Diana Price, only a few years older than Doris Dodge that summer, was assigned to be Benny's dresser. She and another apprentice named David Edgell had little to do that week except escort the comedian to and from the stage. As an apprentice she always addressed her father as "J. P.," not wanting to call him "Dad" in front of the others, and Benny knew Diana only by her first name. He finally learned her full name on the evening her father and Judith Daykin were about to take Benny out to dinner. "I know Diana—are you related to John Price?" said the surprised comedian. "Then you're coming to dinner." Cutting off any anticipated parental objections, he added an ultimatum: "If you don't go, then I don't go!" So Diana got to have dinner with Jack Benny. She remembers that Benny told some good stories that evening, but she doesn't recall whether Benny offered to cover the tip.

Though he didn't get to go to dinner, brother Jock Price ended up with a more tangible memory of Jack Benny's week at Musicarnival. Part of Benny's shtick each evening was to turn to the conductor and ask for his violin, whereupon the instrument would come flying out of the pit, landing on the stage with a frightful crash. "Since he had already made a big thing about his expensive Strad, this always got a big laugh," says Jock. "My job every night, since there obviously was not a whole lot of scene changing going on, was to fix his prop." When the stage manager one evening pronounced the fiddle beyond repair and due for replacement, Jock saw his opportunity. "I asked Mr. Fine [Benny's manager] if I could have it," he says of the battered prop. "So Jack Benny autographed it, and I still have it."

Nearly as legendary as Benny was another headliner closely associated with a musical instrument. Liberace seemed to inspire either the best or the worst from his critics. "I found it hard to reconcile my adverse attitude [with] the thunderous applause and laughter I heard at the Warrensville tent last night," wrote Stan Anderson. "It is a sad commentary on the American scene that a great showman is one who changes from one beaded, shimmering costume to another." The *Press* critic also pronounced himself as "not very impressed with all his jokes about his money and his bank." To Peter Bellamy in the *Plain Dealer,* however, Liberace represented the hope of "a romantic revival and backlash against the Beatles' monotonous beat and Bob Dylan's 'let's slit our throats music.'" Yes, he admitted, "Some of his jokes are terrible, but a few I found quite funny. And it is a joy to watch him work. . . . Everybody ought to see him once. It's an experience."

Of the five book musicals scheduled that summer, the most eagerly anticipated was a new effort, *A Joyful Noise.* Musicarnival, in fact, would be giving the show its world premiere, after which it was to tour ten more summer theaters on its way to a Broadway opening that fall. It was being produced by Edward Padula, whose credits included the highly successful *Bye Bye Birdie.* Oscar Brand and Paul Nassau were responsible for the music and lyrics. Most of the excitement, however, was generated by the casting of the leading role. Padula, who had been looking for a recognized star undaunted by the unorthodox idea of trying out a Broadway show in tent theaters, found his star in John Raitt. Raitt, who had created the role of Billy Bigelow in Rodgers and Hammerstein's *Carousel,* told reporters he had been waiting twenty years for a show like *A Joyful Noise.*

It was a show business musical about the rise of a folk singer from backwoods obscurity to national prominence. Padula, who also wrote the book for the show, described it as a compendium of American song, "from gospel to country music, jazz and folksinging." Raitt delivered the bulk of that message, with eleven of the score's twenty songs and only eight minutes offstage in the entire first act. The company also included two talents that would figure in the future of the American musical, though not for this show. Cast appropriately as a character named Beanpole was a six-and-a-half-foot dancer named Tommy Tune. Choreography was by Michael Bennett, who in due time would create *A Chorus Line.*

A Joyful Noise opened its one-week stand at Musicarnival on June 20, 1966. Peter Bellamy gave the show its most positive notice in the *Plain Dealer.* "The production needs a lot of work, as they say on

Broadway, but it provides considerable charm of melody, song and dance," he reported. "Several of its rousing production numbers stopped the show. . . . The audience loved it." Both Bellamy and Anderson of the *Press* described the work as an amalgam of Padula's *Bye Bye Birdie* with Rodgers and Hammerstein's *Oklahoma!* "Raitt is truly a joyful noise," observed Anderson, "and probably can be heard distinctly over on the neighboring race tracks." Dick Shippy of the *Akron Beacon Journal* weighed in with the most negative review. "Not that bad musicals never find their way to Broadway," he said, "But chances are remote for one this transparently poor."

The Akron critic, unfortunately, proved the best oracle. *A Joyful Noise* limped onto Broadway two months behind schedule in December and folded after only twelve performances. Three years later Musicarnival would present two more pre-Broadway tryouts. *On Time* was a musical revue built around the concept of the generation gap, starring Alfred Drake. Comedienne Martha Raye then appeared as nightclub hostess Texas Guinan in *Hello, Sucker!* with songs by one of Musicarnival's former musical directors, Wilson Stone. Neither show ever made it to Broadway, which pretty much laid to rest the old dream of the tents serving as incubators of new musicals.

Following *A Joyful Noise,* the remainder of the book musicals in the first package year at Musicarnival included *Carousel* with Howard Keel in the John Raitt role, *My Fair Lady* with Anita Gilette, *Oliver!* with John Astin of television's *The Addams Family,* and *How to Succeed in Business without Really Trying* featuring Darryl Hickman. The latter two shows were making their debuts in the tent.

One other show that made an appearance that summer defied categorization: *This Was Burlesque* was a genre in itself. Ann Corio, who once appeared with John Price in the Ring Theater atop the old Allerton Hotel, put together this nostalgic revue featuring veteran baggy-pants comedians such as Dexter Maitland and young strippers such as Miss Dee Light. "Many times I found myself laughing my sides off, even though I knew it wasn't proper, and I've seen the show three times," wrote Bellamy. "To see this," said Anderson of one tassel-twirling ecdysiast, "is to be culturally advanced." Even after a two-week run, Musicarnival hadn't seen the last of *This Was Burlesque.*

It was clearly a new era for Musicarnival, not only onstage but backstage as well. With the resident company disbanded, gone was the hurly-burly of putting a new show together in the day while the previous one was playing at night. "It was never as much fun after that," says John Price, who now became more of a booking agent and theater manager than producer. One thing he still had, however, was his apprentice program, which allowed him to indulge in his passion for proselytizing the glories of Shakespeare. "John Price . . . is very good at Shakespeare, probably one of the ten best Shakespeareans in the country," said one apprentice. "He just picks the wrong hours." Classes on the Bard were generally called after the show on Thursday, running often from midnight to three. ("But soft!" Price might have quoted from *Hamlet,* "methinks I scent the morning air.")

For some of the younger workers, the coming of the package years brought a heady atmosphere of show business glamour. "I was relishing anything going on stage," says Diana Price. "There was the novelty of a new company coming in every week." Diana returned to the tent in its last two years as her father's business manager, where her duties included negotiating contracts, managing personnel, and overseeing acts. "It was one of the most fun jobs I ever had," she remembers. As one of the fellowship students put it, "You get to see the stars without their makeup." They also got to see Phyllis Diller without her jewelry, after the comedienne reported the theft of a quarter-million dollars' worth of baubles, bangles, and beads from her motel. During the production years, it is doubtful whether the entire resident company could have pooled that many gems.

Nearby nightspots tended to replace the old Musicarnival picnic grounds as a gathering place for the stars. Most popular was a lounge called the Blue Grass, located originally in a shopping strip just down Warrensville Center Road and later in a new hotel and restaurant a little farther away on Northfield Road. John Price began having his opening night parties there, and stars such as John Raitt would often

Generally hidden from the audience by the circular valance above Musicarnival's stage, apprentices working the follow spots can be seen in this unique worm's-eye view of the tent's "ceiling." One totally unrehearsed appearance by an apprentice occurred when she lost her balance and fell into the orchestra pit. *Cleveland Press* Collection.

show up after a performance and give impromptu concerts in the lounge. Jack Benny once managed to rattle the staff by coming in and, with his matchless deadpan expression, asking for some corn flakes.

Along with the apprentice program, Musicarnival's Theater School continued into the package years. It was under the direction of former stage manager Judith Daykin, who during the off-season served as stage manager for New York's Paul Taylor Dance Company. Academic affiliation for the six fellowship students was now maintained with the Department of Speech and Dramatic Arts at the newly established Cleveland State University. For their nine credit hours students attended seminars and assumed such theatrical chores as prop handling, scene changing, seating arrangements, and box office procedures. It was described by the *Cleveland Press* in 1969 as the only such program in the country to offer practical experience in professional musical theater.

Apprentices followed essentially the same routine for the experience and a modest stipend rather than credit. "If you think there's glamor in the theater, you're wrong; it's work, cruddy work," commented apprentice Sue Lesnick. "You live in some family's house, tiptoe in, grimy and dirty at 4:00 A.M., can't take a shower because you'd wake everyone up." Though describing it as "the most belittling job in the world," Lesnick stuck with it out of love for the theater. Her application paid off when Carol Lawrence liked the job she did painting the stage so well that she invited the apprentice to join her and husband Robert Goulet for the rest of their tour to supervise floor scenes and care for the couple's two children.

One of the biggest jobs for apprentices during the package years, according to Jock Price, was unloading the shows as they arrived on a truck. Even though some of the biggest visiting stars continued on to participate in the school's seminar program, taking time to share their experiences with the fellowship students and apprentices, nonetheless, Jock feels that the total experience suffered in comparison with the production years, when members of the resident company interfaced with the apprentices "day and night."

While they might see little of the stars during the day, some of the "techies," or technicians, had a unique opportunity to look *down* on the stars during performances. Before one show, Sue Lesnick was assigned to climb one of the poles to the "crow's nest" eighty feet above the stage to open the flap and aerate the tent. The show began before she had a chance to descend, however, making her a captive audience for "one of the worst shows of the season." Three apprentices were intentionally posted in the grid over the stage during each performance to work the follow spots. "We had seat belts, so we wouldn't fall out," explains Jock Price.

Apprentice Cheryl Laser evidently forgot to fasten her seat belt one night in 1969 during a performance of the Wayne Newton show. Training a spotlight on the star during the second act, she lost her balance and plunged twenty-five feet into the orchestra pit. The crash as she landed on music stands, instruments, and a couple of musicians stopped the show quicker than a production number. Peering anxiously into the dimly-lit pit, Newton was relieved to see Laser get up under her own power. "She must be O.K. folks, she's smiling," he announced. It was probably the only time an apprentice received an ovation. Though Laser walked away with only minor cuts and bruises, one of the musicians who helped to cushion her fall suffered a career-threatening lip injury.

One performer the previous season had an even closer brush with disaster. It happened during an appearance by Hetzer's European Circus, which must have felt right at home under Musicarnival's canvas big top. Among the elephant, unicycling, and clown acts was a husband-and-wife illusionist team billed as Nardini and Nadyne. Part of their act called for Nardini to thrust swords into a wooden box occupied by his better half. Something went wrong one night, and Nadyne took a nasty cut from one of Nardini's blades. Calmly she finished the act and then went across Warrensville Center Road to Suburban Community Hospital to have her wound closed with four stitches. From that narrow escape, she returned to the show in time for the second act to escape now from a canvas sack inside a locked trunk. It may have been all in a day's work for her, but it wasn't every night that the staff of Suburban's emergency room got to treat a sword wound.

It would take more than a few stitches to solve some of the challenges of the package years. Just as arena staging had presented a unique set of problems twelve years earlier, the coming of package shows brought its own brand of difficulties. "We attended you[r] show of Aug. 30 and was [sic] very disgusted with the sex act of Corbett Monica," one patron wrote John Price in 1972. He was requesting a refund on four tickets to an upcoming show, because "We do not wish to see anything on the same order." The act in question, a warmup act for the Sergio Franchi Show, riled at least one other Franchi fan who asked, "[W]hy did you spoil the effect upon your cultured intelligent audience with the crude vulgarity of Corbett Monica?" The writer, who had brought guests from Ashtabula to the show, was "afraid they wondered about the 'screening' of your guest, as I also did."

Price had received a similar complaint earlier that summer from a businessman objecting to Alan Drake, who opened Engelbert Humperdinck's show. "The comedian, to my taste, was *revolting—dirty— second rate—vulgar*," he wrote. "*[M]y wife and I will never again attend Musicarnival for any show.* We will not be unwittingly subjected to such trash!" While he could sympathize with the writer's grievance, replied Price, "It is clearly stated in each performer's contract that Musicarnival shall not impose on the material to be presented." He only booked the main star, he added, while "the supporting acts with the show are chosen at the discretion of the star's producer in New York."

There were few, if any, complaints about vulgarity in *This Was Burlesque*, where the audience knew what to expect. Most questions of taste seemed to arise from secondary attractions that were less extensively advertised than the headliners. The following summer, for example, comedian David Steinberg appeared on the same bill with former teenage idol Paul Anka. "To put it bluntly," protested another businessman who said he had been sitting in front of six young girls, "would you like your daughter to hear about 'pre-ejaculations' and 'erections'? Steinberg's entire performance . . . evolved [*sic*] around sex. His type of comedy is expected in many places, but certainly not at *Musicarnival*." Indeed, it was a far cry from the innocent days of *Naughty Marietta*.

Even the audience was occasionally taken to task for offenses against taste. A woman who had attended the Glen Campbell show wrote to complain about "a loud obnoxious drunk" who was brought in by friends in a wheelchair, no less. "They brought their own refreshments—of a liquid variety, in a brown paper bag. . . . Their behavior help[ed] to spoil a fine show for people in our area [of the theater]." Apparently it wasn't an isolated incident. The following night an attendee reported another tipsy patron and friends being supplied during the show from the Musicarnival bar. Though the usherette had cooperated in closing down their pipeline, the writer still thought, "*Too bad* Musicarnival allows their bartenders to dispense booze within the confines of the theater to intoxicated loud-mouthed, bad mannered guests."

But the most general audience complaint during the package years concerned the theater's sound system. There had been acoustical difficulties during the production years, too, but this was a new era with an entirely different hearing problem. "It is 9:30 P.M.," wrote a disgruntled patron in white heat. "[W]e have just arrived home, having left the Mitzi Gaynor show right after the intermission. We didn't leave because of a bad performance—we had to leave because we could no longer tolerate the booming, [ear-]shattering and nerve wracking noise emanating from your loud-speaker system!" A chorus of similar grievances came from other Vegas-style shows. "Throughout the first act we had to sit with our ears plugged in order not to lose our sanity," complained an Engelbert Humperdinck fan. During a Wayne Newton performance, reported one customer, "One lady tried stuffing kleenex in her ears and offered some to her neighbors." Registering a similar gripe, a pair of Tom Jones fans added, "We'll have to stick to records and TV to enjoy his singing."

Believing "when God gave you a voice, you used it," Price had resisted installing any amplification during the early production years until it became clear that the audience behind the actors' backs was missing their lines. Even then, he began with a system designed to reach only to the rear of the actors, while those in front continued to hear the unaided voice. Now, however, he was dealing at least half the time with untrained crooners who had honed their skills in noisy nightclubs. The microphone was not only their umbilical cord; it became an indispensable prop to give them something to do with their hands. Singers no longer had to make themselves heard. That was the soundman's job, and his solution was to simply pump up the amps.

In answer to the numerous complaints, all John Price could say was that Musicarnival had no control over the sound level of visiting shows. "In the performer's contract there is stated an exact level of volume we must produce or fail to keep our obligation to the performer," he explained to the Mitzi Gaynor patrons. Often during shows he had passed on audience grievances to the singer or his technical manager, usually to no avail. "Many times, they have no desire to push down the sound, and we are not able to do so without their permission," he wrote in answer to the Humperdinck complaint.

To some extent it was a generational problem. Patrons of the Robert Goulet show had no gripes about the star but didn't appreciate the volume of a supporting act called the Primo People. "A lady across the stage from us sat through the program with her fingers in her ears," they reported. Two women wrote to say that they, along with many others, had left after the first act of the rock opera *Tommy* in 1973. "We do enjoy many contemporary shows, but not 'ear-shattering Rock,'" they commented. While they realized such fare had "great appeal for the young," they objected to its inclusion in the subscription series.

For most of the Musicarnival audience, however, the star power of the package years more than compensated for some of the drawbacks tied up with the package. "It was a major part of my childhood. What a fun atmosphere it was, waiting at the house to get autographs," says Keith Joseph, who began coming with his mother during the package years. "They would sign them on the porch," he recalls. "Ruby Keeler in *No, No, Nanette* was a big thrill. I got her autograph." The old Grimm farmhouse became the fondly remembered scene of post-performance mixing with the stars. John Price conducted some shy Paul Anka fans there, introduced them to the singer, got their books signed, and then took their pictures. "I had a lovely time just talking with you on the porch and I hope to see you again real soon!" wrote one in appreciation.

To a large extent it was a different audience from that of the production years. "It wasn't just year to year, but show to show," remembers Diana Price. "You would see a different audience for Juliet Prowse than for Engelbert Humperdinck. The Jerry Vales and Robert Goulets all had their own special constituencies." With much of the audience fragmented into such cliques, Musicarnival saw little,

Even John Price was impressed with the showmanship of pianist Liberace, who appeared with his trademark candelabrum. "Look me over," he told his Musicarnival audience. "I didn't get dressed up like this for nothing." Along with other popular acts such as Tom Jones and Engelbert Humperdinck, Liberace attracted his own built-in following to the Warrensville Heights tent. John L. Price Jr. Musicarnival Archives, Cleveland Public Library.

if any, growth in its subscription base. "I'm sure the rise in celebrity culture had a lot to do with it," says Diana.

Liberace was an early example of the trend. Once billed as "Walter Busterkeys," he owed his large television and nightclub following more to his extravagant personality than to his pianistic virtuosity. Making several costume changes per performance, he made one Musicarnival entrance in a bright yellow beaded jacket over white bell-bottoms and frilly lace shirt. "Well, look me over," he told his decidedly matriarchal audience, "I didn't get dressed up like this for nothing." He sported more diamonds and rubies than Phyllis Diller before the great jewelry heist. "Would you like to see the rings?" he asked with an imperial wave of his hand. "You paid for them." For his grand finale Liberace lit up the stage in an electrified suit that Peter Bellamy feared might "blow every fuse in Warrensville Heights."

Such outrageous camping could often disarm the toughest critics, one of whom was Diana Price. "I loved Liberace—I never thought I'd live to see the day I'd say that," she admits. "I thought he was cloying when I saw him on television, but in person he was a real showman." Her opinion was seconded by the master showman himself—her father. "I'll give Liberace this," says John Price, regarding the pianist's theatricality. "Lee had us use the elevator to make his entrance."

The mantle of Liberace was inherited at Musicarnival by a pair of British singers who had appropriated the names of a German composer and an English novel—Engelbert Humperdinck and Tom Jones. The former appeared three times, each visit eagerly anticipated by a fan club calling themselves the "Humperdinck Goils." "We knew if anyone could fill the 'tent,' Enge could," wrote one in thanks to Price, promising an even greater sellout if the singer were booked for the next season. Decidedly *not* a Humperdinck Goil was Wilma Salisbury, who reviewed the concert for the *Plain Dealer*. "A number of gold records say that Humperdinck is a popular singer," she wrote. "But his performance last night at Musicarnival said that he is really just a sex object, beautifully packaged and highly saleable." Chuck Koelble for the *Heights Sun Press* thought the singer had an "off" night, almost completely ignoring his fan clubs and consequently being denied "the standing ovations afforded most of the stars which had preceeded [*sic*] him this year."

If any of his fans had truly been disappointed, Humperdinck made up for it in subsequent summers. He opened the season the following year, and the Humperdinck Goils were back in force. By the time the singer had shed his jacket and tie and unbuttoned the first four buttons of his shirt, observed *Press* critic Frank Hruby, "he could sing in tongues and miss every note, and the audience would scarcely notice." Police were stationed at the foot of the aisles to protect Enge from excessive adulation, but part of every show called for him to select a woman to join him on stage for a personal serenade. On his last visit in 1975 he looked at a young miss from Bedford Heights in the first row and said, "Come up here, Luv." She did, he sang, and then said, "I'm supposed to kiss you now." Said she, "I'm ready." Enge then went beyond the call of duty to give her another song and two more kisses. Following her moment in the spotlight, the demure blonde got the celebrity treatment from the rest of the audience.

They didn't go by a cutesy name like the Humperdinck Goils, but the Tom Jones groupies were scarcely to be outdone in idolatry. Their idol's first Musicarnival engagement in 1972 happened to coincide with his thirty-second birthday, and a number of cards and messages awaited his arrival. "If my poor, old, 1957 Chevy doesn't collapse somewhere on I-71, my friend and I will be in the audience on Saturday," promised one woman from Hamilton, Ohio. Another admirer sent a gift of cigar case, humidor, and cigar clipper. A Parma housewife described herself as a thirty-five-year-old mother of five children and two German shepherds who hadn't gone on a vacation in eighteen years of married life. "My two teenagers, and my husband, play softball so summers to me are nothing but watching baseball games and washing uniforms," she wrote. "If only I could be lucky enough to meet Tom Jones, something exciting would finally have happened to *me*." Her spouse had evidently done his part and gotten her tickets for the late Saturday show; the record fails to reveal whether she got her wish.

With such devoted fans, Jones had a contractual guarantee of one hundred security guards to protect him from being mauled. They formed a human wall to give him an unimpeded entrance from his special trailer to the stage. Chief usher Dick Martin expressed the hope that Musicarnival's female ushers realized that "If the stage is rushed, they're supposed to help ward off the attackers—not join them!" Once on stage, however, the Welsh heartthrob encouraged interaction with his audience. As soon as perspiration began to form on the ends of his curly dark locks, women in the front rows would offer him their hankies to mop his brow, which he would then return with a loud kiss. Some extended more intimate tributes, as enumerated by Bellamy in the *Plain Dealer*; they included a nurse's cap, a size forty-eight bra, and a pair of panties.

Writing the singer afterward in quest of an autograph, a young Cleveland fan related that she hadn't approached the stage for lack of a handkerchief. "I only carry Kleenex with me," she explained. "This was my first attendance at Musicarnival, and I was so over whelmed at the huge tent and especially the crowd—mostly women that were there." A member of the Tom Jones National Fan Club from Pittsburgh expressed its members' appreciation to John Price. They too were impressed—"Not only by Tom, of course, but by the theater itself and the friendliness of everyone we encountered there. . . . Would also like to compliment the Musicarnival on the lighting set-up and the good sound system." Should she ever move to Cleveland, she told Price, "the first thing I would do would be to buy a season subscription!"

A teacher from Sheffield Lake wrote Price that autumn in joyous anticipation of "THE SECOND COMING" of the Jones boy. There was a second coming in 1973 and a third in 1975, but a scheduled appearance in 1974 had to be canceled when the singer contracted laryngitis and acute bronchitis. Musicarnival had a rare dark week that summer, causing business manager Diana Price to take out cancellation insurance for the 1975 coming of Tom Jones.

Neither Liberace, Humperdinck, nor Jones, however, attracted the annual following of *This Was Burlesque* at Musicarnival. Taken together, the aforementioned trio played the tent a total of eight weeks, a record easily outdistanced by the seventeen weeks in ten seasons by *This Was Burlesque*. "We had the equivalent of an entire season with nothing but burlesque," sums up John Price. It attracted forty thousand people to its first two-week stand in 1966. When Price cut it down to a single week's run two years later, he had to schedule an extra performance to satisfy the demand. Thereafter he booked the show for two one-week runs a season. Like a pair of showy bookends, *This Was Burlesque* would often open and close the tent each summer.

A former stripper, who never took it all off herself, Ann Corio put the show together in 1962 as a nostalgic tribute to an entertainment in decline. Her timing was obviously right, as *This Was Burlesque* proved a hit in sophisticated New York before, seemingly perpetually, taking to the road. Adding authenticity to Corio's reproduction, veteran candy butcher Arthur Von Weigand worked the stage and aisles between the acts. For local radio critic Howard Wertheimer, it brought back memories of "the old days" at the Star Burlesque on Euclid Avenue and the Empire Theatre on Huron Road. "Perhaps one of its appeals is that it reminds every man in the audience of his youth and of the time that he saw his first burlesque show," wrote Bellamy after a dozen or so viewings. "It may also suggest to him a less painfully sophisticated era where nudity was a novelty, not a drug on the market."

In the increasingly permissive atmosphere of the 1960s, often amazed reviewers tended to stress the comparative innocence of the older form. "The perenially [sic] young and shapely Miss Corio . . . as usual presides over the comic, bawdy revels with the innocence of a Sunday school teacher who would run screaming to the Watch and Ward Society if she had the slightest suspicion that anything risque was happening," observed Bellamy of another viewing. "Everything's done for nostalgia in the show," Corio told an interviewer for the *Cleveland Press*. "We've got terribly corny jokes, the pie-in-the-face gag, seltzer water and no four-letter words except 'damn' and 'hell.'" But as she would coyly tell the audience, "If we didn't get a little naughty, you wouldn't be packed in here like this."

Among those packed in were a surprising number of women—a good half of the audience at times, according to some reviewers. There were even senior citizen discount nights, but though Price put an "adults only" label on ads for the show, the kids weren't always left at home. "I used to torture my mother every year to take me," says Keith Joseph. "I was the only ten-year-old who loved burlesque." With comics such as former television star Jerry Lester taking the shaving cream pies in the face, the show offered more than mere prurient interest. "The racy, earthy humor kids sex in a zany way," wrote Dick Wootten in the *Cleveland Press*. "There is no obsession with the obscene or erotic."

Still, it wouldn't have been burlesque without such strippers as Tami Roche, billed as "the only exotic who can twirl four tassels si-

In an impressive display of histrionic versatility, statuesque Tami Roche assumed the persona of Miss Liberty in a patriotic tableau for *This Was Burlesque*. John L. Price Jr. Musicarnival Archives, Cleveland Public Library.

multaneously, 'Two Fore' and 'Two Aft.'" Assessing her art, Bellamy wrote, "Tami (Tassels) Roche has brought tassel-twirling, originated by the late Carrie Finnell, to its finest flower. Her figure is truly voluptuous in abundance and design." More than just a pretty figure, however, Roche displayed her versatility by impersonating a presumably tasselless Statue of Liberty in the show's first-act finale. (A pair of her pasties unaccountably turned up in the Musicarnival Archives, where they were accessioned and exhibited as "Tami Roche's theatrical accoutrements.")

In later editions of the revue, tassel-twirling Tami was succeeded by Luna, "Goddess of Love and Fire." Tassels were too tame for Luna, who twirled a pair of flaming torches as part of her act as she danced in the midst of a blazing fire. Described as "a Haitian voodoo dancer who practices and believes in the occult, witchcraft, black magic and spiritualism," she averred that supernatural forces protected her from the flames. When performing in the States, claimed the program notes, Luna was barred from including the culmination of her act in the West Indies, where she would decapitate a live chicken and drink its blood. Even without this grisly denouement, says John Price, "She was a pistol."

During one late Saturday performance, Luna more closely resembled a loose cannon when one of the flaming tips of her torches flew off its handle and into the audience. It landed in the lap of a lady sitting in the front row in a kelly-green pants suit. "Of course, fire's no joke in the theater," says Price, who remembers combustible fluid spilling out all over the stage. To the rescue rushed usher Deborah Weiler, who somehow found a wet towel and used it to extinguish the burning torch while others mopped up the spilled fluid. House manager Kenneth Albers checked on the woman and her husband, who were uninjured and not too badly shaken. "They were very pleasant and seemed to be a bit embarassed [sic] by the fuss that was being made over them," reported Albers, who commended Weiler for "averting what was a potentially explosive situation." Arranging to compensate the victim for the cleaning and repairing of her singed suit, Albers was convinced that the usher's "quick action . . . saved Musicarnival a good deal of pain and embarassment [sic]."

Though few boasted bombshells comparable to Luna, most of the shows of the package years had their memorable moments. Had Luna flipped her torch during Peggy Fleming's show, there would have been no problem. The Musicarnival stage was covered by a twenty-seven-by-thirty-five-foot ice rink for the former Olympic skating champion. Singer Sammy Davis Jr. lived up to his Rat Pack image by taking a bourbon break on stage. "Robert Goulet would flirt with my mother," remembers Keith Joseph. Danish pianist Victor Borge brought his comedy routine near the end of the Lyndon Johnson administration and told of his interview with the president. "He picked me up by the ears and called me a Great Dane," quipped the solemn-visaged humorist.

Nor were the book musicals without their memories. The opening of *Promises, Promises* in 1972 was made memorable by veteran song and dance man Donald O'Connor. As a musical version of the Billy Wilder movie *The Apartment,* the show itself was distinguished mainly for the Burt Bacharach tune, "I'll Never Fall in Love Again." It wasn't necessarily a showstopper in itself, but a heavy downpour during the middle of that number at Musicarnival had the same effect. After a few minutes' rain delay, O'Connor took matters into his own hands and whispered some instructions to the orchestra. Out of the pit floated the strains of (what else?) "Singing in the Rain," as O'Connor broke into a soft shoe to the song linked to his name from the movie of the same title. That was followed by a chorus of "Tea for Two" until the rain let up. "It's all right," O'Connor called as apprentices appeared to mop up the puddles from leaks in the tent, "I've followed elephants." *Press* columnist Don Robertson, who deplored "cheaply bestowed" standing ovations, made an exception to the one given O'Connor that night as a fitting tribute to a trouper.

Star turns in package musicals, then, had their compensations for the loss of the stock company from the production years. Musicarnival audiences got to see Janis Paige in *Mame,* Chita Rivera in *Sweet Charity,* and Carol Lawrence in *Funny Girl* and *The Sound of Music.* "To sum it up, Miss Rivera is one of the great ones and 'Sweet Charity' is a triumphant vehicle for her, as well as a highly entertaining show," wrote Bellamy in the *Plain Dealer.* Clevelanders also had a chance to see stars reprise roles they had made famous. Carol Channing appeared in *Lorelei,* a revised version of *Gentlemen Prefer Blondes.* Irving Jacobson recreated the role of Sancho Panza, which

Although Musicarnival had first done *Gypsy* during the production years, Angela Lansbury, seen here in "Rose's Turn," made the show an artistic high point of the package years. John L. Price Jr. Musicarnival Archives, Cleveland Public Library.

he had played in the original cast of *Man of La Mancha*. Georgio Tozzi, who had done the singing for Rossano Brazzi in the movie version, was seen as well as heard as Emile de Becque in *South Pacific*.

Despite another opening night rain delay, Tammy Grimes emerged triumphant in the title role of *The Unsinkable Molly Brown*.

Unfortunately Cleveland didn't have an opportunity to see John Raitt as Billy Bigelow, since he was still trying out *A Joyful Noise* when Musicarnival did *Carousel* with Howard Keel in the role originated by Bonnie's dad. Raitt did return later in such shows as *On a Clear Day You Can See Forever* and *Kismet*. He also played his first Harold Hill in the tent's *The Music Man*. Diana Price recalls him as "always so nice, so genial—no false ego." Another show she remembers fondly, even though it didn't do well at the box office, was *Gypsy* with Angela Lansbury. "The only thing that dates this 1959 show is the fact that it has so much good music, such literate lyrics and a book with so much bite in it," said Tony Mastroianni of the *Press*. "Angela Lansbury in *Gypsy* was the best for pure professionalism and talent," seconds Keith Joseph. "She was magnificent." It came before Lansbury's television breakthrough as amateur sleuth Jessica Fletcher, however, which may explain the show's failure to click.

Finally there were Musicarnival's "Fiddlers Three." Opening on Broadway in 1964, Harnick and Bock's *Fiddler on the Roof* eclipsed *My Fair Lady, Oklahoma!* and *Hello, Dolly!* over the next few years on its way to a record run of 3,242 performances. Musicarnival finally got it in 1971—twice. At the beginning of the season it came with Metropolitan Opera baritone Robert Merrill in the lead. "Merrill is not only a splendid singer; he is an actor and comedian of considerable abilities," said Don Robertson in a radio review, "and he brings all these qualities to the role of Tevye, a Jewish farmer in Czarist Russia who is the central character in this show." Another Metropolitan star, tenor Jan Peerce, was the Tevye in the *Fiddler* company that closed out that season. "There have been better actors in the role, but Peerce is quite good enough and not nearly so wooden as he has been in some operatic roles," wrote Mastroianni. "As an actor he is a better Tevia [*sic*] than he is a Rudolfo. As a singer he is quite capable of doing both."

Merrill's appearance had prompted a couple of audience complaints, not for what he sang but for what he didn't sing. Both letters objected, quite vehemently, to the cutting of a duet between Tevye and his wife Golde. "In my opinion the duet of the song 'Do you love me['] was to be the highlight of the performance," wrote one. "By your decision, you took the glow of the evening away from us, as well as the surrounding people in our section." In reply, Price noted that shows had been cut without objection in the past, especially on Saturdays with two evening shows scheduled and a parking lot to be cleared in between. "FIDDLER is such a masterpiece that it's impossible to make a delicate cutting of it," he admitted. "As a matter of fact, when was the last time you sat through an uncut version of HAMLET on ANY night?" he asked, perhaps a bit irrelevantly. "I doubt that you asked for your money back when at least THIRTY MINUTES was cut from the greatest dramatic classic in the English language."

There were no complaints when the third Fiddler arrived four years later. This one happened to be Zero Mostel, the comic genius who had created Tevye in the show's original cast. Cleveland had seen Luther Adler recreate the role in the touring company at Music Hall, but this was its only chance to see the master himself. "Well, it's official. Zero Mostel 'is' Tevye," Emerson Batdorff wrote in his *Plain Dealer* review. "All those other fellows we have enjoyed through the years in the role in 'Fiddler on the Roof' have been frauds." Tony Mastroianni came to essentially the same conclusion. "More than any other Tevye, Mostel brings out all the humor in the role," he said. "He has a speaking voice with a built-in shrug. He mugs shamelessly, puts in bits of business that are surely his own. . . . But his sense of rightness is unerring and he never takes away from the show." Musicarnival audiences endorsed that opinion with a one-week record attendance of 17,000.

"By that time he was sleepwalking through it," remembers Diana Price, "but he was still better than any of the others." Emerson Batdorff described Mostel spotting Carol Channing in the audience as he made one of his exits: "He stopped. His mouth opened like a fish planning to eat alphabet soup. His eyes bulged possibly an inch. Then he went on about his business." There was a pair of steel doors on the Musicarnival dressing room that visiting stars had taken to signing in the manner of the fabled autographed curtain of the Hanna Theatre. Zero, whose paintings had hung in the Museum of Modern Art, tagged the door with a ribald drawing.

Coming near the end of the package years, Mostel's *Fiddler* may have been Musicarnival's last hurrah. There were fewer and fewer book musicals; *No, No, Nanette* was the only one of the breed in 1974. "The young people wanted rock and roll," says Price, who began booking rock groups such as Led Zeppelin in 1969 in place of the Sunday jazz concerts. Members of one group made headlines in 1971 when they were arrested at Hopkins Airport on suspicion of drug possession. "It certainly does not say much for your Musicarnival when you sign up music groups who are dope addicts," wrote one incensed citizen from Cuyahoga Falls. "For the good of society, places like yours should perhaps be put out of business." "I am sorry to hear that you believe that we knowingly signed a contract with 'dope addicts,'" Price replied dryly. "Thank you for your interest in our programs." During the rock acts, he later told an interviewer, he generally retreated to his office and listened to WCLV, the classical music station—"real loud."

John Price didn't need Bob Dylan to tell him the times were a' changing.

5

Striking the Tent

It had become traditional by 1975 for Ann Corio to appear early in the Musicarnival season with *This Was Burlesque*. Top banana Pinky Lee provided the comedy that year along with Maxie Furman in baggy-pants bits and Harry Conley, who at eighty-eight still got laughs out of the hoary "dumb wife" routine. Luna made a return appearance as "Goddess of Love and Fire," though one reviewer surmised that she was "probably neither a Haitian voodoo dancer nor a ritual drinker of chicken blood, as the program notes declare." At any rate, she lit the audience's fire only in a figurative sense this time around. Another single-named exotic, Donovan, stood statuesquely in for Miss Liberty in an early salute to the nation's bicentennial. It was mistress of ceremonies Corio who nearly stole the show on opening night, however, with the seemingly innocuous ad lib that, in view of the theater's imminent closing, this would be her last appearance at Musicarnival.

Though Corio later stated that she had been "misinformed," her slip of the tongue sparked rumors that persisted over Musicarnival all season, like flashes of heat lightning in the summer sky. "We are not yet ready to fold our tent and silently steal away," John Price assured Tony Mastroianni of the *Cleveland Press*. While admitting that ideas about a new theater and possibly a new location were under consideration, he affirmed that the show would go on in the meantime at the old stand for at least another season or two. With a pretax profit approaching $200,000, the season before last (1973) had been the best in the tent's twenty-year history.

But that had been the year before the debut in 1974 of the Front Row Theater. Described as the first new permanent theater in Greater Cleveland since the 1927 Cleveland Play House, the new facility opened on July 5 with a program headlined by Sammy Davis Jr. Its investors included shopping center developer Dominic Visconti and Nate Dolan, a former part owner of the Cleveland Indians. Nate's son Lawrence, a future owner of the Indians, was named general manager. Located a few miles up interstate I-271 in Highland Heights, the Front Row posed a direct challenge to Musicarnival. It not only had a circular stage, but one that revolved. Capacity was 3,200, several hundred more than could be accommodated under Price's tent.

With its slick $3 million plant complete with champagne bar, the Front Row was custom-tailored for the coming to maturity of the "baby boomers." It was a generation raised on television—some might say *by* television—and attuned to the musical beat of rock and roll. Despite a handful of exceptions such as the "tribal rock musical" *Hair*, the new pop music wasn't readily compatible with the scoring of book musicals. Its monochromic expressiveness was ill-suited to interpret the complexities of a well-rounded story; its performers were often at sea without the security blankets of mikes and electric guitars. In recognition of the change in popular taste, the Front Row eschewed book musicals in favor of Vegas-style acts such as Wayne Newton, Liberace, and Steve Lawrence and Eydie Gorme.

It was precisely in this type of entertainment that the Front Row was competing toe-to-toe with Musicarnival. In going after the hottest acts, the newer theater apparently had the advantage of unlimited financial backing. According to Diana Price, Musicarnival habitually negotiated its Vegas acts such as Tom Jones on a 90–10 percentage basis: the theater would take the first $40,000 of the gross, after which the performer would get 90 percent. "The Front Row was not buying talent on percentage cuts but offering guarantees," she explains. "I remember discussing this with [New York booking agent] Jack Lenny—he wasn't able to get acts for Musicarnival because they were going to the Front Row." Among the defectors were Engelbert Humperdinck, Sergio Franchi, and Glen Campbell.

The immediate success of the Front Row only added to speculation over the future of Musicarnival. When the tent's lease had come up for renewal in 1974, there were rumors that developer Edward J. DeBartolo, owner of Thistledown, might find other uses for that corner of the racetrack grounds. For 1975 the lease was extended only on a yearly basis, with an increase in rent from $25,000 to a minimum of $40,000. Price had been thinking for some time about a new Musicarnival in a different location. What had been farmland when the theater opened was now crowded with apartments, hospitals, and a new shopping mall built by DeBartolo on the nearby grounds of the former Randall Park racetrack. There had been talk of a theater-in-the-round seating 4,500 as part of the latter complex, but DeBartolo opted for an additional department store instead. Nick Mileti, says Price, had invited his participation in the Coliseum he opened in Richfield in 1974, but Price couldn't see how to fit the kind of theater he wanted into the huge sports complex.

Six weeks into the 1975 season, Ron Weskind in the *Ashland Times-Gazette* reported a falling off of attendance at Musicarnival. "The reasons why attendance may be declining this year are many," wrote Weskind, citing a current economic recession and increased competition from the Front Row and the Coliseum. "Musicarnival also changed its format back to the original idea of staging Broadway shows along with the night club acts," he added. "Many of the acts that had annually returned to Musicarnival went instead this year to the Front Row." Price had booked three package shows back-to-back early in the season. While Zero Mostel broke the house record with *Fiddler on the Roof,* *Variety* later reported that business was only fair for Carol Channing in *Lorelei,* and *Gypsy* had bombed, despite Angela Lansbury.

Pictured by Jim Herron, Zero Mostel finally gave Cleveland a chance to see the original Tevye in *Fiddler on the Roof* for Musicarnival's last season. Although he broke the house record for a single week, it wasn't enough to save the tent. *Cleveland Press,* June 20, 1975.

Broadway musicals weren't entirely the problem. "Even Tom Jones, a top draw, failed to do so, we are told," Ron Weskind had written.

One more Broadway show opened in the tent that season. Although it might not make anyone's list of greatest musicals, *Grease* would eventually break the Broadway-record run of *Fiddler on the Roof*. Its popularity in the cynical 1970s may have stemmed from the fact that it offered nothing more challenging than a reprise of high school life in the early days of rock and roll. "In another decade or so, the show probably won't work, but for now the nostalgia gimmick is a good excuse to revive the era on stage," wrote Chris Columbi for the *Plain Dealer*. "Last night's audience welcomed that revival with the laughter of recognition of an era gratefully gotten through."

Musicarnival had been born in the time frame of *Grease*, which lent irony to the fact that the show unexpectedly was fated to be the final attraction on its main stage. It opened in mid-August, and during the one-week run news was received of the cancellation of two shows scheduled for later in the season. One was country singer Buck Owens; the other was a revival of the 1920s musical *Good News* with Don Ameche and Alice Faye. With nothing available to fill the gaps, Price called a special meeting of the Musicarnival board at the Union Club. Reporting an operating loss to date of $70,000, Diana Price as business manager estimated additional losses of $20,000–$28,000 over the remainder of the season. In the face of such figures, as well as the uncertain future of the Musicarnival lease, the directors voted to terminate the season at the end of that week's run of *Grease*. Among the remaining shows thereby cancelled was the return engagement of *This Was Burlesque*. Ann Corio had it right the first time.

"The final performances of GREASE this Saturday at 7 and 10:30 P.M. may well be the last ever to play the circular stage of the big blue tent, since plans are underway to build a new Musicarnival Theatre in the near future, but at a different location," stated a press release covering the decision. "Well over two million patrons over the past twenty-two summers have made the Musicarnival tent in Warrensville Heights an area landmark, and many of the greatest stars have performed on its circular stage. . . . Musicarnival gratefully acknowledges the support of its patrons and subscribers, many of whom have been coming to Musicarnival since its inception in 1954."

Elaborating on the formal statement for the local press, Price cited the roles played by the economy and the rental increase. "We were forced to raise the prices because of a rise in our rent and the exorbitant demands of the stars and their agents," he disclosed. Attendance had been good at lower prices on Mondays and Tuesdays, he noted, concluding that "Actually, we should have been lowering our prices in this depressed economy." Price denied that the decline in box office receipts had anything to do with the quality of the product. "We had some of the best shows in the game and we got 'money' reviews on them. . . . It really turned me off [on] the local theater-going public," he ended on a rare note of pessimism.

Post-mortems were conducted by various theater pundits. Music critic Frank Hruby in the *Press* saw Musicarnival's passing as part of the inevitable evolutionary cycle of theaters. Just as Price's tent had supplanted Cain Park with its canvas shelter and ample parking, so was it destined in time to yield to newer ventures offering even more in the way of "creature comforts." "When Musicarnival opened 22 years ago," observed Donna Chernin in the *Plain Dealer*, "the idea of attending a rustic outdoor theater and sitting in canvas chairs was exciting and invigorating." Such upstart competitors as the Front Row, the Coliseum, and the Cleveland Orchestra's Blossom Music Center, she implied, had taken the edge off the novelty of Musicarnival. "As people have grown more affluent and spoiled, they want luxuries like air conditioning, a modern building, upholstered seats and a paved parking lot," added Stu Levin, who had served Price as assistant to the producer.

In retrospect, Diana Price remembers Musicarnival as "always a profitable venture" but burdened by the old millstone of the debt from the Palm Beach operation. "It never really got out from under it," she recalls. Her father puts a share of the blame on the changing times. "It was rock and roll, the steady declination in public taste," maintains John Price. "Unless a musical was fresh off Broadway, or really hot, they just wouldn't come." Keith Joseph, the youthful Musicarnival patron who later became a theater critic, concurs with that judgment. "Musicals are not as much a part of pop culture as they were thirty years ago," he says. "Basically, they couldn't afford to do musicals anymore, and there was no room for variety shows when the Front Row took over."

Contemporaries nevertheless lamented the passing of an institution. "When Johnny Price founded Musicarnival in 1954, Cleveland had practically no top-notch entertainment outside downtown and none at all in the summertime," editorialized the *Cleveland Press.* "Tens of thousands of Clevelanders who enjoyed Musicarnival over the years wish him success. The man who kept entertainment alive in Cleveland deserves it." Noting the "close-at-hand rapport between audience and those on the circular stage," the *Plain Dealer* concluded that "Performers appreciated Musicarnival no less than patrons. . . . Mutual feelings of excitement and enjoyment usually prevailed." Warrensville Heights Mayor Raymond J. Grabow regretted the loss not only of the theater's annual admission tax of $35,000–$40,000, but also of the "positive image" Musicarnival had brought to the suburb. On the possibility of using the tent for future rock concerts, Grabow said he would welcome the idea if supervised by Price, who had "always run a professional and orderly performance."

So the final curtain—figuratively speaking, since Musicarnival had never used such a device on its circular stage—came down on the late-Saturday-evening performance of *Grease,* technically in the wee hours of Sunday, August 17, 1975. It wasn't quite the last act under the tent, since a pair of Children's Theatre productions was still on the boards. *You're a Good Man, Charlie Brown* played the weekend after *Grease,* followed by *Adventures in Wonderland* on August 28–29. Then it really was "curtains" for Musicarnival, as Price held a tent sale on Saturday, August 30. Included in the memorabilia of twenty-two years offered to the public were theater programs, posters, publicity photos, costumes, fake flowers and other props, office supplies, a washer and dryer, and Musicarnival tee shirts. Although the tent itself wasn't sold, neither was it ever used again, whether for rock concerts or a stop-gap season preceding any new theater.

M·U·S·I·C·A·R·N·I·V·A·L

Cleveland's Famous Summer Musical Theatre-in-the-Round

Grease

B'WAY'S LONGEST RUNNING SHOW!

1975 SEASON
Great Stars in
Great Musical Shows

It wasn't planned that way, but *Grease* was fated to be the last main stage attraction at Musicarnival. The musical took a nostalgic look at the 1950s—the era when the tent had first been raised. John L. Price Jr. Musicarnival Archives, Cleveland Public Library.

Price's resident company, of course, had long been disbanded and scattered among the varied branches of show business. Several of them turned up a few seasons after the production years in a hit off-Broadway musical called *Your Own Thing*. Former Musicarnival director Don Driver was responsible for the book of this rock version of Shakespeare's *Twelfth Night*. Doubling as director, he cast former Musicarnival players Marian Mercer as Olivia and Imogene Bliss and Igors Gavon in minor roles. Otto Pirchner, Driver's understudy as director at Musicarnival, now served his predecessor as assistant stage manager. *Your Own Thing* became the first off-Broadway production to win the Critics Circle Award for best musical.

Driver had already achieved a Tony nomination for his direction of a revival of Peter Weiss' *Marat/Sade* on Broadway, where he cast Imogene Bliss as one of the asylum inmates. "A lot of what I learned I know from Musicarnival," he told a reporter. "You can't minimize the freedom John Price gave me to try many new things." Later he directed Henry Fonda in a revival of *Our Town* and Dustin Hoffman in Murray Schisgal's *Jimmy Shine*. In movies, Driver provided the screenplay and directed an adaptation of Desmond Morris's *The Naked Ape*. He died of AIDS in New York at the age of sixty-five. His protégé, Otto Pirchner, shared a similar fate, achieving a career in stage direction but also succumbing to AIDS.

Musicarnival's original director, Bill Boehm, survived his two successors. He was still acting on occasion in the tent when Price loaned him the facility to audition children for a Christmas concert in 1964. Looking for forty young singers, Boehm was pleasantly surprised when 150 answered his call. He organized them on a permanent basis as the Singing Angels, a performing chorus that eventually grew to 160 voices. Some of their early successes came at Musicarnival, where they appeared both in their own show and as a warm-up act for the Wayne Newton show. Newton also featured them on one of his television shows, and the group won an Emmy for their own Christmas television special in 1970. As their fame spread, they performed at the White House and undertook tours to such locales as Germany, Russia, and China. Boehm remained as their director into the twenty-first century.

Other Musicarnival alumni made their marks in show business. Judith Daykin, stage manager and softball relief artist, left the tent to become director of the Chagrin Valley Little Theatre. In time she reached the pinnacle of musical theater production as president and executive director of the New York City Center. There is a legend among Musicarnival old timers that Ernie Horvath fibbed about his age to land a part in the *Cinderella* premiere. As a cofounder of Cleveland Ballet, Horvath would eventually be staging his own premieres. John-Michael Tebelak, who painted scenery as a Musicarnival apprentice, later wrote a modern treatment of the New Testament while a student at Carnegie-Mellon University. Produced as *Godspell,* it enjoyed highly successful runs both on Broadway and off-Broadway. Not surprisingly, a former Musicarnival actress had an important part in the revival of Cleveland's Playhouse Square. Providence Hollander was one of a quartet of performers that staved off the wrecking ball in a record-setting run of *Jacques Brel Is Alive and Living in Paris* in the State Theatre lobby.

As for the Price family, Connie and John eventually divorced but remained on amicable terms. She kept active in civic and little-theater affairs until her death in 1997. Philip and Mikey, the two nontheatrical children, remained in the Cleveland area, Mikey in Willoughby Hills and Philip as a veterinarian in Eastlake. Jock Price replaced a show technician in the package production of *Sweet Charity* when it left Musicarnival. After touring with a couple of more shows, he attended the University of Iowa and did radio work in Erie, Pennsylvania. Eventually he settled in West Virginia, where he served one governor as press secretary, became involved with the Jaycees, and continues to care for Jack Benny's violin. Next to her father, Diana Price maintained the closest involvement with theater. From apprentice she moved up to publicity and finally business manager at Musicarnival. After the tent folded she spent two seasons working for Music Fair, a hard-topped theater-in-the-round in

Baltimore. Returning to Cleveland, she has served as business manager for Cleveland Ballet, the Cleveland Play House, and *Northern Ohio Live*. Diana has also become involved in the Shakespeare authorship controversy, another enthusiasm shared with her father. He has served as president of the Shakespeare Oxford Society; her contribution was the recent publication of *Shakespeare's Unorthodox Biography*, an anti-Stratfordian book that maintains a neutral stance on the identity of the true author of Shakespeare's plays.

John Price continued dreaming of a new theater for several years after folding the tent. He told Peter Bellamy at the time that he wanted a multipurpose complex capable of accommodating experimental theater, children's theater, film festivals, chamber music, with maybe a motel and swimming pool thrown in. It would seat more than the Front Row and have the ability to convert itself from an arena to a proscenium stage at a moment's notice. All he needed was about $6 million, estimated the man who had started Musicarnival on $120,000. A few years later he was still talking of such a theater, a facility able to embrace "all forms of art . . . theater, opera, ballet, orchestras and even exhibitions." Price envisioned a location with "ample parking facilities" in the coming growth area of Strongsville. Despite a mushrooming price tag of $15 million, experimental and children's theater were still vital parts of the plan. "I know that is the only way for the future; otherwise the arts, as we know them today, will gradually die," he warned.

Meanwhile Price maintained a highly visible presence on the local theater scene. He performed the title role of Ben Jonson's *Volpone* under Judith Daykin at Chagrin Valley Little Theatre, and for Larry Vincent at Cuyahoga Community College he played Uncle Sid opposite Vivian Blaine's Aunt Lily in *Take Me Along*. The Lakewood Little Theatre gave him a chance to direct one of his favorites, Loesser's *Guys and Dolls*. Price has also become famed for his solo dramatic readings. For better than half a century he has given annual readings of Charles Dickens's *A Christmas Carol* in venues ranging from Notre Dame University to Plymouth, England. Less regular, but equally well

John Price's hopes of resurrecting Musicarnival in a new location were never fulfilled. The tent was struck for the last time in August 1975. John L. Price Jr. Musicarnival Archives, Cleveland Public Library.

remembered, are his readings of Ernest L. Thayer's "Casey at the Bat." "It's the most overlooked creative piece of theater in this town," says Bill Boehm. "He's inimitable, absolutely inimitable."

In the end, Price's visionary theater never materialized. There was little if any margin for profit for the kind of theater he wanted to do. Even if he had been able to swing financing, he probably would have been limited to producing packaged shows. For Price, the "glory years" at Musicarnival had always been the first twelve production years when he had his own stock company. "Up until then [the change to package shows] I never worked a day in my life," he says. "Then it just wasn't fun anymore."

A couple of years after the tent, however, something turned up that was fun again, when Price was invited to become executive director of the Northern Ohio Opera Association. This was the organization that sponsored the annual visits of the Metropolitan Opera Company to Cleveland, which made Price for at least one week a year the biggest impresario in Ohio. It also gave him a bully pulpit for promoting his goal of taking some of the starch out of the "stuffed-shirt atmosphere" of opera. "I don't want people to come to the opera like bums," he told a reporter. "They should at least wash behind their ears. But I'd rather have them come as bums than not at all." And come they did, as Price personally barked the splendors of the "M-m-m-m-ighty Met!" in radio commercials over nine seasons. One fringe benefit of the job was a renewal of his association with Beverly Sills, who appeared in Massenet's *Thaïs* in one season and Donizetti's *Don Pasquale* the following year. Of the former, Price relished telling about the woman who called about getting tickets to see "Beverly Sills in Thighs."

A year after overseeing the moving of the Met from Public Hall to Playhouse Square—and a year before the end of the Met's tours—Price retired from the opera job. He was living in a condo overlooking the Flats, practically in the shadow of John Ellsler's old Academy of Music, which Price remembers exploring shortly before its demolition. (*That* must have stirred up a company of theater ghosts!) Hearing of the establishment of a D-Day Museum, he gathered up all the war mementos he had once been ordered to destroy and sent them to New Orleans. The bulk of his Musicarnival records was turned over at the same time to the Cleveland Public Library.

• • •

A full generation after dimming its lights, Musicarnival is still remembered as a unique chapter in Cleveland's theatrical history. With a backward glance to the days of John Ellsler, it was the last of the city's permanent, commercial stock companies. Looking toward the future, it introduced a new, challenging form of theater to a mass audience. Full theater-in-the-round, Musicarnival-style, may have been an ephemeral theatrical phase, but local contemporary companies, from Dobama to the Play House Baxter Stage, still follow the arena plan at least three-quarters of the way. "It was a brand of theater new to the area, and it did not take Musicarnival long to take Cleveland by storm," recalls Bill Boehm. "Everybody took the seats, the holes in the canvas in stride. It demanded a new dimension in performance. It was a wonderful time, a glorious adventure."

More than anything, Musicarnival will be remembered for what it did best in its "glory days," as a venue for professional performances of the American musical. Most of the classics of the golden age (1943–1964) were given their turn on its circular stage, generally for the first time locally since the visits of the touring companies from Broadway. A good portion of the audiences now packing Playhouse Square for touring revivals of *South Pacific, Show Boat, Kiss Me, Kate,* and *The Sound of Music* are renewing acquaintances first made in the rustic setting of the Thistledown grounds. Along with these newer musicals, the tent also gave its audiences a generous sampling of the older operettas that had been the staple of Cain Park, from *Naughty Marietta* to *The Student Prince.*

Price's "operatic venture" of the late 1950s represents only a miniscule slice of Musicarnival's entire repertoire, but it looms large in any assessment of its artistic achievement. Due to inspired casting as well as the soprano's subsequent local marriage, Clevelanders had a unique opportunity to see and hear Beverly Sills on the threshold of her brilliant career. She gave a total of nearly fifty performances in the tent, which wasn't far from the number of her later appearances at the Met. If Price ultimately lost money on his five productions, it was par for the course for that most extravagant of all the arts. Justifiably, he always counted them as among Musicarnival's finest moments.

Another contribution, unseen by the general public, was Musicarnival's education program. Once again John Price had trod in the footsteps of John Ellsler, whose Academy of Music gained a national reputation as a "school of the drama" for training such future stars as Clara Morris. On-the-job training was necessary in Ellsler's day, when theater arts were considered beneath the dignity of college curriculums. There were countless drama schools and departments by Price's day, but Musicarnival offered practical experience in an area of theater often neglected in the regular dramatic curriculum. It may have been an unusual concern for a commercial theater, but John Price always had at least one eye cocked on posterity.

As Frank Hruby had observed, theatrical trends were cyclical affairs. The Front Row Theater, which in some respects had replaced Musicarnival, enjoyed a slightly shorter lifespan of twenty years before relinquishing its bookings to the revitalized Playhouse Square Center downtown. In its five theaters, Playhouse Square today accommodates both Vegas-style entertainments and touring Broadway megamusicals. An hour's drive south of Cleveland, a summer repertory troupe puts on revivals of operettas in an intimate theater in Wooster. A revived Cain Park has been producing annually one "big" musical in its Evans Amphitheater and a more intimate one in the Alma Theater, many under the direction of musical theater specialist Victoria Bussert.

All are the spiritual successors of Musicarnival, which in its day did it all. "I think we upped the standards for local productions when there hadn't been much of that," says Price, whose claim was generally verified by local and visiting critics. In the words of Tony Mastroianni of the *Cleveland Press,* "No one did it quite so well as the company Price put together when Musicarnival was in its youthful prime." At its best it was indeed an eminent standard; even at its rare less-than-best, Musicarnival always put on a good show.

Appendix A: Musicarnival Production List
The Production Years, 1954–1965

1954
Oklahoma!
The New Moon
Roberta
The Student Prince
Finian's Rainbow
Show Boat
Annie Get Your Gun
Carousel
The Desert Song

1955
Kiss Me, Kate
South Pacific
Die Fledermaus
Brigadoon
Wish You Were Here (LP)
Guys and Dolls

1956
The King and I
Plain and Fancy (LP)
Call Me Madam
The Merry Widow
Carmen
Wonderful Town
Kismet

1957
The Pajama Game
Tosca
South Pacific
Gentlemen Prefer Blondes
Can-Can
Song of Norway
Silk Stockings
Damn Yankees
South Pacific

1958

Oklahoma!
The Most Happy Fella
Annie Get Your Gun
Show Boat
Finian's Rainbow
Peter Pan
Guys and Dolls
The Ballad of Baby Doe (MP)
Carousel
Porgy and Bess (PS)

1959

The King and I
The Boy Friend
The Great Waltz
Wish You Were Here
Kismet
Li'l Abner (LP)
The Student Prince
Bells Are Ringing (LP)

1960

West Side Story (PS)
Anything Goes
The Vagabond King
Pal Joey
Fanny
Naughty Marietta
The Student Prince
Redhead (LP)

1961

Cinderella (WSP)
The Red Mill
Take Me Along (LP)
Paint Your Wagon
High Button Shoes
Die Fledermaus
Bloomer Girl
South Pacific

1962

The Music Man
Flower Drum Song
Bye Bye Birdie
Fiorello!
The Desert Song
Gypsy
Do Re Mi (LP)

1963

Carnival
Can-Can
Gentlemen Prefer Blondes
The Merry Widow
Wildcat
The Unsinkable Molly Brown

1964

The Sound of Music
Camelot
The Boys from Syracuse
Kiss Me, Kate
Milk and Honey
My Fair Lady

1965

The Sound of Music
Show Boat
110 in the Shade (LP)
The Music Man
South Pacific
Sing Out, Sweet Land
*A Funny Thing Happened on the
    Way to the Forum*

WSP	World Stage Premiere
MP	Midwest Premiere
LP	Local Premiere
PS	Package Show

Appendix B: Musicarnival Production List
The Package Years, 1966–1975

1966
Belafonte
The Mike Douglas Show
A Joyful Noise (WP)
Carousel
This Was Burlesque
My Fair Lady
Jerry Lewis
Jack Benny
The King Family
Oliver!
*How to Succeed in Business
    Without Really Trying*
Liberace
Robert Goulet in Concert

1967
This Was Burlesque
*On a Clear Day You Can See
    Forever*
The Wayne Newton Show
Funny Girl
The Johnny Mathis Show
The John Davidson Show
Sweet Charity
Bravo Burlesque!
The Phyllis Diller Show

1968
J. Hetzler's European Circus
Borge Presents Borge
Sid Caesar and Imogene Coca
The Jerry Vale Show
This Was Burlesque
Liberace

South Pacific
The John Davidson Show
The Sound of Music
The Music Man
The Frankie Laine Show
The Fantasticks

1969
The Jerry Vale Show
This Was Burlesque
The Student Prince
Mame
On Time (PB)
The Phyllis Diller Show
Hello, Sucker! (PB)
Barefoot in the Park
The Wayne Newton Show
The Johnny Mathis Show
This Was Burlesque

1970
The Wayne Newton Show
This Was Burlesque
The Robert Goulet Show
Man of La Mancha
I Do! I Do!
The Jerry Vale Show
Enzo Stuarti and Pat Cooper
This Was Burlesque
Cabaret
The John Davidson Show

1971
Fiddler on the Roof
Jerry Lewis
The Sammy Davis Jr. Show
This Was Burlesque
Hello, Dolly!
The Robert Goulet Show
Kismet
The Sergio Franchi Show
The Vicki Carr Show
The Sound of Music
This Was Burlesque
Fiddler on the Roof

1972
Tom Jones
The Wayne Newton Show
This Was Burlesque
Sandler and Young
The Mitzi Gaynor Show
Engelbert Humperdinck
The Eddy Arnold Show
The Jerry Vale Show
The Peggy Fleming Show
The Al Martino Show
Jesus Christ Superstar
The Sergio Franchi Show
1776
Promises, Promises
This Was Burlesque

1973

Engelbert Humperdinck
This Was Burlesque
Bill Cosby
Sandler and Young
Tom Jones
The Glen Campbell Show
Dionne Warwick
Paul Anka and David Steinberg
The Carol Lawrence Show
The Unsinkable Molly Brown
The Mitzi Gaynor Show
Tommy
The Totie Fields Show
The Connie Stevens Show

1974

No, No, Nanette
This Was Burlesque
The Sergio Franchi Show
The Loretta Lynn Show
Engelbert Humperdinck
The Jerry Vale Show

Juliet Prowse
Sandler and Young
Gladys Knight and The Pips
The Mitzi Gaynor Show
Paul Anka
This Was Burlesque

1975

Ben Vereen and Melba Moore
This Was Burlesque
Tom Jones
Fiddler on the Roof
Lorelei
Gypsy
Joel Grey
Patti Page and George Gobel
Al Green
Grease

WP   World Premiere
 PB   Pre-Broadway Tryout
Italics denote book musicals

Bibliographic Note

By far, the greatest concentration of materials about the history of Musicarnival is to be found in the John L. Price Jr. Musicarnival Archives, housed in the literature department in the main branch of the Cleveland Public Library. According to a preliminary inventory, the principal assets of the collection include 30,000 color slides, 11,000 black-and-white photographs, 200 audio tapes, 32 scrapbooks, 50 linear feet of files, 10 volumes of programs, 4 volumes of board minutes, and miscellanea, including architectural drawings, scene designs, and props. Especially helpful in the preparation of this study were the scrapbooks, which are already available on microfilm. Three of the most valuable single sources from the Archives proved to be a transcript of John Price's lecture to the Musicarnival School on "Problems of a Producer," Price's own account of the beginning of Musicarnival prepared as background for the CPL Musicarnival exhibit in 2001, and a long feature on Price by Peter Bellamy in the *Cleveland Plain Dealer* of July 28, 1974.

Another potential source of Musicarnival material consists of records donated by John Price to the Western Reserve Historical Society in 1998 but unfortunately not yet organized for scholarly research. An estimated 150 shelf feet of material includes posters, photographs, business records, and audio recordings. A large percentage of this collection, however, pertains to the Northern Ohio Opera Association headed by Price after Musicarnival. One unique Musicarnival item is the set of four dressing room doors autographed by visiting stars largely from the package years.

A small handful of secondary sources may also be of interest to the general reader. For Musicarnival's place in local theatrical history, see this author's *Showtime in Cleveland: The Rise of a Regional Theater Center* (Kent, Ohio: Kent State University Press, 2001). The early history of Musicarnival's direct predecessor, including much material on John Price, may be found in Dina Rees Evans's *Cain Park Theatre: The Halcyon Years* (Cleveland: Halcyon, 1980). Beverly Sills makes mention of Musicarnival in both of her autobiographies, *Bubbles: A Self-Portrait* (Indianapolis: Bobbs-Merrill, 1976) and, with Lawrence Linderman, *Beverly: An Autobiography* (New York: Bantam, 1987).

Index